MILLION-DOLLAR FRAUDS

By
Gary McKechnie and Nancy Howell

The Institute of Internal Auditors

ISBN 0-89413-402-7
98330 04/98
First Printing

Contents

Executive Summary

Million-Dollar Frauds covers a wide range of capital market fraud cases. Due to the losses incurred, many of these cases received detailed coverage by major magazines, newspapers, and television networks. In this book, we examine the events leading up to the commitment of fraud as well as the consequences and ramifications suffered by the perpetrators and their companies. Each case contains a warning for employers — fraud can occur anywhere at anytime. By examining these cases collectively, you may detect a psychological pattern that appears in the "rogue employee" as well as lax controls within your organization that may need to be strengthened.

To make this book entertaining as well as educational, it was written in a style utilizing layman's terms and a chronological narrative to appeal to readers who may not even work within a financial institution. The thrill of following a case from a minor indiscretion to the loss of billions of dollars is undeniable, and readers will have the opportunity to see what elements existed in each scenario.

Since internal auditors cannot detect every person committing fraud, the responsibility is one that falls upon all of us. By understanding the motivation behind and the execution of capital market fraud, we trust this will enable you and your employees to detect the early warning signs of fraud possibly being committed within your own organization.

About the Authors

Gary McKechnie and Nancy Howell, a husband and wife writing team, both graduated from the University of Central Florida with degrees in Radio/Television. In 1990 they embarked as freelance writers and have written and produced videos for numerous clients, including Disney University Management Seminars, the Greater Orlando Aviation Authority, and Spaceport USA. In 1996 they received a Telly Award for a humorous training film on Control Design and Risk Assessment, written and produced for The Institute of Internal Auditors.

McKechnie and Howell also write travel and feature articles for publications, including the *Washington Post, Miami Herald, Denver Post, Orlando Magazine, Orlando Sentinel, Ft. Lauderdale Sun-Sentinel, Chicago Tribune, New Orleans Times-Picayune,* Continental Airlines' *Profiles*, United Airlines' *Hemispheres*, and *Fodor's Florida.*

Acknowledgments

We greatly appreciate the support of Credit Lyonnais' Stephen Doherty in the preparation of this book. The subject of capital fraud often lends itself to levels of information as vast as the sums of money diverted by rogue employees. He was extremely helpful in directing us to cases that provided a well-balanced cross-section of fraud that has occurred in financial institutions, local governments, and in Eastern Europe. We trust that readers will find every case intriguing.

We also appreciate the assistance of those in the Educational Products division of The Institute of Internal Auditors, in particular Elaine McIntosh, Hope Smarrito, and Michelle Goembel.

Introduction

When asked why he robbed banks, Willie Sutton responded with remarkable logic: "Because that's where the money is."

● ●

For Sutton and his contemporaries, robbing banks was a physical affair. Cash was kept in vaults and withdrawn at the barrel of a gun. Safeguarding assets involved building stronger vaults and hiring more guards.

Things were simpler then. Within minutes of a robbery, bankers knew how much money was gone. The public knew that good guys ran banks and bad guys robbed them — it was easy to tell the two apart. Today, however, things are not so clear. Protecting assets is no longer a matter of locking the vault. Dillinger wannabes have traded pistols for computers, as financial institutions face repeated attacks by a global network of determined cybercriminals.

The transition from a cash-based economy to electronic commerce has increased the speed and flexibility with which assets may be moved around the globe. Expanding economies and market globalization have demanded more reliance on capital markets to sustain growth. Newer and more complex financial instruments are being created to meet constantly changing business needs. Trading has moved from a means of financial intermediation to a means unto itself. To produce strategic profits, old-line product producers are now placing increased emphasis on trading in the capital markets and place their fates in the hands of Wall Street wizards to successfully navigate these markets.

Yet one constant has survived decades of technological change: greed. The quest for instant wealth has motivated criminals since the days of Willie Sutton, but the stakes have risen substantially. In his 30-year career, Sutton put his life on the line with each robbery and managed to steal roughly $2 million. In the 1990s Joseph Jett destroyed the operating viability of Kidder-Peabody by single-handedly creating $350 million in false profits. It has become increasingly difficult to separate the good guys from the bad since bank presidents (Charles Keating), star employees (Nicholas Leeson), and long-admired patriarchs (Robert Citron) have narrowed the once wide chasm between respect and reproach.

It may be unfair to compare decades-old crimes with today's cases of capital fraud, so let's examine some recent figures provided by the National White Collar Crime Center (NWCCC) located in Richmond, Virginia. A 1994 Federal Bureau of Investigation study comparing crimes revealed that the annual cost of street crimes — burglary, robbery, larceny, auto theft, and arson — was estimated at $13 billion. However, the broad area of white collar crime — fraud, forgery, embezzlement, and counterfeiting — cost Americans roughly $415 billion, or 32 times as much as the total cost of street crime.

Similar figures compiled by the NWCCC itself estimates annual losses in specific areas associated with white collar crime:

- Employee Theft (embezzlement & pilferage): $5 billion to $435 billion
- Corporate Tax Fraud: $7 billion to $50 billion
- Computer Related/High Tech Crimes: $100 million to $40 billion
- Corporate Financial Crimes (organizational/occupational fraud and deception, antitrust violations, bribery, corruption, price fixing, restraint of trade): $200 billion to $565 billion
- Savings & Loan, Stock Brokerage (Collective Embezzlements): $8 billion to $25 billion

Although these figures are approximations (no exact figures exist) they are supported by a three-year study by the Association of Certified Fraud Examiners which concluded that U.S. businesses and governments lose $400 billion annually through petty theft and major fraud. On average, companies lose nine dollars per day per employee, which means by year's end their losses will average six percent of an organization's annual revenue.

So who is committing these crimes? In 75 percent of fraud cases, the losses are incurred by college educated, professional males who steal more than four times the amount taken by their female counterparts. In terms of responsibility, senior executives (whose tenure has resulted in a greater amount of trust) "out-fraud" junior employees by a 28-to-1 ratio.

Admittedly, not all senior executives — or junior employees — start out as would-be Dillingers. In many cases, these financial ne'er-do-wells were led astray by ego. Relatively minor errors were transformed into insurmountable losses when Daiwa's Iguchi and Barings' Leeson chose not to admit their mistakes, but to hide them. Consider also California's Robert Citron whose 24 years of success as county treasurer convinced him he could accurately outguess the markets.

Perhaps the greater hubris of all, however, is found in executive boardrooms. In almost every case of major capital market fraud, senior management has chosen not to believe that such things could happen on their watch. Occasionally, explicit signs that faulty internal controls are leading their companies to economic disaster are ignored since the prospect of profitable returns blinds management to obvious dangers.

Having been involved with auditing financial institutions for 17 years, I have watched these cases of fraud unfold year after year and recognized common threads that run through these multimillion (and multibillion) dollar disasters. In a "lessons to be learned" presentation, I have often appeared before senior business managers and informed them of the warning signs preceding the revelation of fraud. The reactions were invariably the same. First, there is snickering at the company that permits such lax controls to exist. Then, as the details of each case are presented, one by one, the smiles usually disappear and the laughter subsides. The scenarios soon became recognizable to the senior managers who realize that the same situations can occur within their own companies.

So what warning signs should you look for? In the cases profiled in this book, you'll learn that fraud follows common patterns: employees gain the trust of their employers; they take advantage of a lack of control; increased profits prompt superiors to ignore internal regulations; the employees hide their losses until it leads to financial collapse and public embarrassment; and, finally, their superiors deny any previous knowledge of wrongdoing.

Other red flags you might recognize are employees who refuse to take vacations, a seeming virtuous act performed only to prevent detection. Also look for employees who live far beyond their means. CIA spy Aldrich Ames earned $70,000 a year, but owned a home worth $500,000 and wore $2,000 suits.

Since these conditions appear regularly in audit and control consultant reports, when taken separately none would likely herald impending danger. But should they remain unaddressed, the foundation is laid for the next level of fraud.

This is why it must be stressed that, by virtue of their position and the responsibilities attached to it, management must be willing to accept the fact that fraud can occur within their ranks. Unfortunately, many times senior managers confronted with the revelation of fraud have the same knee-jerk reaction: reject the facts and portray their organization as a victim of a rogue employee. When the smoke clears, however, the facts consistently reveal that the fault lies not with their stars, but with themselves. In case after case, management seems willing to turn a blind eye to the lax controls in light of the outstanding profits being made.

Whether it is an organization of 30 or 30,000, senior management and the board of directors have a duty to exercise due professional care in making informed judgments and taking reasonable actions regarding the management of organizational risk. Granted, "rogue employees" may be primarily to blame but the corporate culture that does little to promote or strengthen controls has developed a management style that has abdicated its basic responsibilities.

History suggests that markets will continue to evolve; the financial services industry will become more electronically dependent; and new organizations will develop innovative ways to capture their share of the profits. Amid these changes, however, one thing will stay constant: human nature and the greed and egotism associated with it. Likewise, management will continue to ignore suggestions of impropriety in light of profitability. Audit comments will go unheeded until the odds turn against some unfortunate firm which could be profiled in the future. In Washington, Congress will rattle the sabers of legislation and the story will continue...

As George Santayana wrote in his *Life of Reason*, "Those who cannot remember the past are condemned to repeat it."

Stephen Doherty
November 1997

JOSEPH JETT
"Jett Crashes on Wall Street"

He saw himself as a superman among Wall Street traders: a handsome, intelligent, driven man determined to make it in the financial world. Perhaps that air of confidence is why no one took the time to verify Joseph Jett's resume and work history. But by hiring him, the brokerage firm of Kidder Peabody Group, Inc. lost more than they bargained for.

More than a quarter of a billion dollars.

• •

On Wall Street, Orlando Joseph Jett was recognized as the quintessential Renaissance man. The 36-year-old sportsman, philosopher, theater buff, and music aficionado had also earned a reputation as one of Kidder Peabody Group, Inc.'s most talented traders.

By all accounts, a man in his position had to have one hell of a solid background. Just a glance at Jett's resume proved he was the man to make trades. Within the last decade, his resume showed he had received a master of business administration from Harvard and a degree from Massachusetts Institute of Technology. His work experience included a position as senior process engineer for General Electric (GE), where he was named "top performer" and promoted to advanced production engineer.[1]

Not shown on his resume was the day in June 1984 when he was taken away from GE's Selkirk, New Jersey, plastics plant in handcuffs. Just a misunderstanding about a bad check, he explained.[2]

But learning about new ways to make plastics was no longer exotic enough for this man of the world. Joseph Jett wanted to learn new methods of making money. He left GE in 1985 and entered Harvard Business School. Although he managed to complete his coursework, he left without a diploma in hand. Instead of paying his last semester's tuition, Jett chose to spend the money on a trip to China.[3]

Despite his missing diploma, Jett managed to land a job on Wall Street. In 1987 Morgan Stanley & Co. hired the articulate 29-year-old as a junior trader in mortgage-backed securities. He also learned arbitrage trading and how to devise trading strategies while in their structured-finance group. But somehow, the magnetism of Jett's personality failed to impress his superiors. Following two years of lackluster efforts, Jett became a casualty of a broad round of layoffs.

After several months, he took a pay cut to work for CS First Boston, and returned to his role of packaging mortgage-backed securities. Repeating his lackadaisical work history, Jett proved he wasn't what this firm had hoped for either and was fired in 1990. He did leave his mark behind, however. Jett's dismissal was so sudden he didn't have time to erase a computer file that contained a list of women and their sexual talents.[4]

For eight months, Jett was on the skids. Unemployed, he fell behind in his $850-a-month rent. Then in mid 1991 fortune smiled upon the unemployed trader. He spotted an ad seeking a qualified candidate to develop software for trading desks on Wall Street. His credentials led him to Kidder Peabody.[5]

Ironically, the investment firm was now owned by GE, Jett's first employer. Although GE was regarded as a company content to make huge profits in the unglamorous world of industrial machinery, nearly everyone agreed that spending $602 million for Kidder in 1986 was a logical move. When combined with well-oiled GE Capital Services Inc., the ensuing synergy would lead to GE's dominance of the financial services market. So what if they didn't really understand Kidder Peabody's business? Good management is good management and what worked for GE would work for Kidder Peabody.[6]

Although Jett's background pointed toward experience in mortgage securities, his enthusiasm, high energy level, and positive manner made him an ideal candidate for a position on the government bond desk.[7]

His placement was endorsed by Edward Cerullo, chief of Kidder Peabody's fixed income department. A former high school math teacher and school bus driver, Cerullo had arrived at Kidder Peabody in 1979 on the strength of an MBA from Columbia University. He had already earned a favorable reputation on Wall Street, and now it was Jett's turn.

Behind the scenes something else was working in Jett's favor. Kidder had recently been named in a breach of contract lawsuit filed by a former black trader. Under pressure by GE to hire and promote minorities, some suspect that Jett's arrival at Kidder was a matter of being in the right place at the right time.

Regardless of how he entered the front door, Jett was determined to correct the character flaws that had resulted in less than spectacular work histories.[8] He arrived earlier and stayed later than most other employees. But longer hours didn't translate into a comprehensive understanding of his job responsibilities.

During his first few months, Jett was losing money so rapidly that his colleagues suspected he wasn't fully familiar with the market.[9] If Jett overbid on a stock, a fellow trader would usually take him aside and suggest he correct his mistakes before he embarrassed himself in front of his customers. To Jett's credit, he tried not to forget the lesson. He also didn't forget the people who doubted his abilities.

Within months, colleagues Hugh Bush and Monica Flanagan noticed discrepancies on Jett's trades and accused him of illegally "mismarking" or "inflating" the prices of the securities he held.[10] To Jett, it rekindled the anger he felt as a child in Wickliffe, Ohio, when classmates beat him up for being too smart. But now his colleagues' accusations stoked Jett's belief that he was being persecuted for his race.

Cerullo, however, was colorblind. He liked Jett and the profits he was making. So in April 1992, when Hugh Bush again raised questions of Jett "mismarking" trading positions, did Cerullo investigate? No. Did the hierarchy within Kidder determine there was just cause to question their star trader? Not exactly. Jett defended himself by turning in an audiotape of Bush making a phone call in search of other employment. Cerullo fired Bush and the matter was forgotten.[11]

When compared to the mounting profits, the loss of one employee seemed trivial. During Jett's first full year on the desk, he had earned revenues of $30 million — nearly double the previous record of $16 million.[12] By 1993 that total had more than quadrupled to $140 million which accounted for nearly 30 percent of the fixed income department's $439 million in annual operating profit.[13] What's more impressive is the fact that Jett was able to generate these profits by trading Treasury strips, a commodity considered to be a very low margin area of the fixed-income business. Astounded by the results, Cerullo promoted Jett to head of the government bond desk, a move that left other traders scratching their heads and grumbling under their breath.

But who else was capable of laying such huge profits at the altar of Kidder Peabody Group, Inc? Actually, nearly anyone who didn't mind breaking the law.

Sometime after his arrival in 1991 Jett began initiating a series of phony transactions that involved "strips" and "recons." The process worked this way: brokers can deliver whole bonds to the Federal Reserve Bank and receive back discounted "stripped" securities. Likewise, brokers can also deliver "strips" to the Fed and receive back whole bonds in a process called reconstituting, or "recon." The effect is roughly the same as trading four quarters for a dollar, although as discounted securities, strips will accrue interest which make them more valuable in the future than in the present.

This was all Jett needed to know.

Within Kidder Peabody's trade processing system, exchanges with the Fed were treated as conventional purchase and sales transactions. But a glitch on Jett's computer allowed him to show profits before his trades had been completed. When Jett started to establish forward trades as far as three months in advance, the system recognized the transactions as profits for the company.[14] When it came time to settle, Jett would simply roll the transactions over and earn even more make-believe money. No one had any reason to suspect something was awry: according to his confirmation slips, the trades were being processed on behalf of the Federal Reserve. In reality, Jett was depositing them into an artificial account.[15]

So why was Jett willing to take such risks? Aside from the obvious recognition as a super trader, it was the hefty salary plus bonus that reached $9 million in 1993.[16] Ironically, it was his sheer volume of trades that kept Jett above reproach. When compared to the $1.7 trillion in trades he transacted that year, $9 million was a mere pittance. Who would argue that he didn't deserve it? Not Cerullo. His income amounted to about $20 million — in large part due to the business Jett was hustling.[17]

But this time Jett may have overplayed his hand. Although massive figures like that bypassed Cerullo, they caught the attention of auditors. After twice visiting the government bond trading desk, the auditors were convinced by Jett that everything was on the level.

Had they looked a little closer, they may have discovered that Jett was putting $350 million in phony profits into Kidder and GE ledgers at a time when he had lost $90 million through his legitimate trades. Despite all the dollar signs, there was no sign of real cash. Internal statements didn't separate profits from the sale of securities ("realized" profits) and profits from increases in the value of the securities ("unrealized" profits held in the firm's portfolio). In other words, no one knew exactly how Jett was making money — or where it was.

Although he may have fooled the auditors, Jett continued to arouse the suspicions of fellow traders. Jett's commanding physical presence combined with his growing financial clout gave him an increased sense of power. If queried on a sensitive topic, Jett's rebuttal "Are you questioning me?" became an effective defense mechanism for ending conversations.

Bruised egos and accountability aside, Kidder senior executives recognized Jett's achievements in January 1994 by presenting him with the Chairman's Award as their star trader of 1993. In just over two years, Jett had single-handedly turned a desk that traditionally generated around $20 million a year into one that produced revenues of $140 million.

As far as Kidder could see, Jett was taking them to the stratospheres of profitable trading.

But it was all about to come crashing down to earth.

In the first quarter of 1994 his unbelievable earnings of roughly *$100 million* raised a red flag the size of Kansas. This also raised the eyebrows of Kidder attorneys, who began to review Jett's ledgers and asked that he reduce the amount of trades. Jett complied by selling off some of his real positions — a move that temporarily pacified his interrogators. But by April, the truth was staring them in the face: Jett's fortune was based on phantom profits but his $90 million losses were all too real. Now even Cerullo was becoming suspicious.

For two weeks Jett stalled his boss with financial double talk until Cerullo had had enough and pushed his point home. He asked Jett to meet with several Kidder Peabody executives to explain where the money had gone. Put on the spot, Jett demonstrated that he was not as skilled at coming up with a real explanation as he was at generating phantom profits. His rambling excuses fell on deaf ears.[18]

On April 16, 1994, Jett was fired. The following day Kidder Peabody disclosed the phony government bond trading scheme. It's doubtful anyone thought to call former employee Hugh Bush and offer their belated thanks for raising the first red flag a few years ago, but his suspicions had proven to be true.

It must have seemed like deja vu to Cerullo. Just three years earlier he had paid a $5,000 fine for failing to supervise a trader who had engineered unauthorized bond transactions.[19]

As in most cases of fraud, finger pointing became a form of high art. In the following months, parallel universes were created. In Jett's world the bottom line was racism and Cerullo was the mastermind who ordered Jett to make trades as part of an elaborate scheme to generate profits.

On Cerullo's planet, however, Joseph Jett was a rogue trader who engaged in phantom trades that prompted GE to report a $210 million loss.

Outsiders managed to balance their criticisms. While Jett had demonstrated he was indeed taking great risks and hiding his losses, it was generally agreed that as his boss, Cerullo should have understood Jett's positions and questioned him when the profits had grown abnormally large. Rallying to Cerullo's defense, however, Kidder Peabody Chief Executive Michael A. Carpenter insisted the company's internal controls were good, it's just that Jett's ruse was better. Besides, he added, there were no red flags raised between Jett's profits and the real trades on the books; they had grown gradually and "there didn't seem to be anything terribly out of line."

Outsiders suggested this cavalier claim of ignorance was shielding one of the primary problems: that as long as profits were being generated, high-rolling traders like Jett were given free rein to cut their own deals.

Perhaps this shouldn't have come as a surprise. Carpenter's background wasn't in securities, but as a GE management consultant. And rather than report to his equal at GE Capital (with whom he didn't get along), Carpenter instead reported to his friend, GE Chairman John Welch.

Considering the difference in products, some economists even suggested it would have been easier to mix oil and water than the traditional financial operations of GE Capital and the exotic investments of Kidder Peabody.

Amid the punches and counterpunches, former Securities & Exchange Commission Enforcement Chief Gary Lynch began wading through the morass. He had already taken down Ivan Boesky and Michael Milken, and now he had to find the culprit at Kidder Peabody.

After reviewing trading books and taking testimony from dozens of employees, he presented an 85-page report commissioned by GE. He found that Kidder Peabody suffered from "lax oversight" and "poor judgments" which enabled Jett to show $350 million in phony trading profits from 1991 to 1994.

This didn't sit well with GE Chairman John Welch. He viewed his company as a tightly run ship, but now that Kidder had sprung a $210 million leak, Welch decided it was time to abandon ship and sold the flagging firm to Paine Webber. In the process, more than 2,200 Kidder Peabody employees were cut loose.

Suits and countersuits filled the courts. Unfortunately, Jett's defamation suit against five Kidder Peabody executives was as unsuccessful as his trading career. In March 1997 New York State Supreme Court Judge Stuart Cohen said Jett had failed to specify what the five executives had done to defame him.

Sometimes you just can't win.

*Actually, sometimes you *can* win. In 1996, Jett managed to score a minor victory when an arbitration panel agreed that Jett actually believed his trades were making money.

References

[1]Siconolfi, Michael, "Saga of Kidder's Jett: Sudden Downfall of an Aggressive Wall Street Trader," *Wall Street Journal*, Apr. 19, 1994, A3.

[2]Freedman, Alix M., and Cohen, Laurie P., "Jett's Passage: How A Kidder Trader Stumbled Upward Before Scandal Struck," *Wall Street Journal*, Jun. 3, 1994, A6.

[3]Ibid.

[4]Ibid.

[5]Ibid.

[6]Siconolfi, Michael, op. cit., A12.

[7]Freedman, Alix M., and Cohen, Laurie P., op. cit., A6.

[8]Ibid.

[9]Cohen, Laurie; Freedman, Alix M.; and Power, William, "Growing Mess: Kidder's No. 2 Man Comes Under Scrutiny in Trading Scandal," *Wall Street Journal*, May 2, 1994, A8.

[10]Freedman, Alix M., and Cohen, Laurie P., op. cit., A6.

[11]Cohen, Laurie, et al., op. cit., A8.

[12]Freedman, Alix M., and Cohen, Laurie P., op. cit., A6.

[13]Ibid.

[14]Cohen, Laurie, et al., op. cit., A8.

[15]Siconolfi, Michael, op. cit., A3.

[16]Freedman, Alix M., and Cohen, Laurie P., op. cit., A6.

[17]Cohen, Laurie, et al., op. cit., A3.

[18]Siconolfi, Michael, op. cit., A12.

[19]Freedman, Alix M.; Cohen, Laurie P.; and Siconolfi, Michael, "Yidder Trading Controls Drew Scrutiny Well Before Jett," *Wall Street Journal*, May 6, 1994, C1.

TOSHIHIDE IGUCHI
"Dedicated Deception"

In July 1995 Toshihide Iguchi was hard at work. It was nothing unusual for the dedicated employee. Daiwa Bank, Ltd. was the 13th largest bank in the world and Iguchi was one of its most devoted traders. But today he wasn't doing his typical job of trading millions of dollars. Instead, he was writing a letter of confession that would let his superiors know that over the past 11 years, he had lost the company $1.1 billion.

• •

Forty-four-year-old Toshihide Iguchi impressed his friends, colleagues, and acquaintances as being unusually mediocre. Having graduated from high school in Japan as an average student, he immigrated to America to study in 1970. Sadly, Iguchi's so-so scholastic abilities accompanied him to Southwest Missouri State University where he excelled on the cheerleading squad, but toiled for five years to earn a degree in psychology.[1]

After college, Iguchi took a job selling used cars. It's doubtful that any of the other Mazda salespeople were in awe of his education; still, the diploma reminded him that he did have potential. By 1976 Iguchi was ready to make a clear break with his past. Having married while at college, he moved his family to New York where he landed a position as a clerk in the securities deposit department at Daiwa Bank, Ltd. For Iguchi, this was a chance to prove himself. Big time.[2]

Daiwa was the 10th largest bank in Japan and the 13th largest in the world.[3] In the early 1980s Wall Street was pumping out profits, and banks like Daiwa were ready to grab some easy money.

Iguchi was ready to grab the brass ring. In 1984, with eight years of loyal service behind him, he was promoted to the position of bond trader while continuing his duties as a clerk. With increased responsibility, Iguchi now had a greater opportunity for advancement.

Although Iguchi's Japanese bosses didn't seem to understand bond trading, he apparently did. And he liked it. They trusted him and left him alone to make small, safe trades.

Then he lost $50,000.

Although his specialty was trading Treasury bonds, recognized by Wall Street wizards as being the safest, most foolproof commodity, Iguchi made an error predicting the direction interest rates would take. The resulting $50,000 bath represented only about one one-millionth of Daiwa's nearly $200 billion in assets,[4] but to Iguchi it threatened his first real success. No one really needed to know about this trivial error, did they? Not at least as far as Iguchi was concerned. Disappointed and anxious, he wasn't about to let this do him in. It was only a matter of time until he could cover the shortage and no one would be the wiser.

As he continued making trades (and racking up mistake after hidden mistake), he garnered higher profile promotions and eventually became executive vice president and head of U.S. government bond trading.

But every success has a price. While his career was forging ahead, his personal life was falling apart and his marriage broke up in 1987. Still, he had a secure job, was treated with respect by his superiors, and was well liked by colleagues who gave him friendly nicknames like 'Tosh,' 'Toshy,' and 'Mr. 52,' due to his habit of trading in odd amounts like $52 million.[5] Life was good for Iguchi.

But as months passed, Iguchi realized that like most things in his life, making up the loss wasn't as easy as he thought it would be. By now, the bad debts were slowly taking on a life of their own and soon the trader was forced to learn a new skill.

Forgery.

Since Iguchi was both a clerk and a trader, he was in the optimum position to enter the front office and make his own trades, then step into the back office to record them.[6] He answered only to himself. Iguchi alone controlled the key to Daiwa's money, but he couldn't control whether he'd make a profit or lose a fortune. He usually lost.

Still no one knew. As the millions mounted, Iguchi would simply dip into Daiwa's customer accounts, sell the bonds, and then forge documents to make it appear as if the sale had been authorized. That's it. He was clear and his tracks were covered.[7] Since no one was following up on Iguchi's books (accounts were held at the Bankers Trust New York Corp.), it made no difference whether the documents were authentic or not. To his superiors, the bottom line remained the same: Iguchi was a dedicated, trustworthy employee who understood bond trading and regularly earned the company an average of $4 million in profits year after year.[8]

In reality, Iguchi was part Nick Leeson and part Robert Citron. Like Leeson, Iguchi's imminent downfall began with a minor error (in Leeson's case it was trying to cover for a novice trader's £20,000 error). And similarly, Iguchi was responsible for both front and back offices and assumed this power would allow him to correct any mistakes.

Yet unlike Leeson, Iguchi wasn't in it for the money. He didn't care if he ever owned a yacht, joined a country club, or drove a Porsche. In this regard, he more closely resembled Orange County Treasurer Robert Citron, whose frugal ways repeatedly got him reelected to office. Aside from his impressive $300,000 home, Iguchi maintained a low profile. To his neighbors, he was merely a figure who came and went. To his coworkers, he was a youthful-looking man who wore inexpensive suits, golfed, and loved to watch the Mets. Unfortunately, he also shared Citron's inability to admit that he didn't fully grasp the intricacies of certain financial devices — a trait that would prove fatal.

Meanwhile, Iguchi had convinced himself that he could correct that nagging $50,000 error that was costing Daiwa millions of dollars every week. No matter what it took, he would remain at the controls. Lucky for him, Daiwa proved to be an accommodating, if unsuspecting, coconspirator.

Iguchi's first advantage was that Daiwa had hired him in the United States. Had he been hired in Japan and relocated to New

York, company policy dictated that he'd be rotated back to Japan within three to five years. Instead, he was considered to be a long-term, local hire and not subject to relocation. And why would Daiwa executives want to relocate someone like Iguchi? He was fluent in Japanese as well as English, had a thorough understanding of trading, was completely dedicated, and seldom took a day off. Ever since he was promoted to trader, he couldn't stand to be away from his office. While other colleagues looked forward to taking a two-week vacation, Iguchi would only leave for two or three days at a time before he'd hurry back to his desk.[9]

The lack of suspicion was indicative of Daiwa's corporate culture — management placed great trust on the ability of traders to regulate themselves. One unusual aspect of Iguchi's trades, however, was the fact that his transactions were recorded on paper, not electronically. For a multibillion-dollar company to allow a trader to use this archaic method of accounting was an open invitation to deception and fraud.

But it was the result of a previous banking scandal that would eventually be his downfall.

Although he had nothing to do with the collapse of the Bank of Credit & Commerce International (BCCI) in 1991, Iguchi suffered from the corrective measures that were implemented by federal regulators to prevent bankers from inflating accounts and falsifying records. The Foreign Bank Supervision Enhancement Act of 1991 gave U.S. authorities greater latitude to police banks such as Daiwa.[10]

As a result of the heightened scrutiny, in 1993 Daiwa moved their trading operations to midtown Manhattan, leaving Iguchi stranded in the back office on Wall Street. Although the banking regulators made it clear that Iguchi was no longer allowed to work both offices, Daiwa apparently depended on Iguchi and it was suspected that he was still calling the shots in both locations.

For two more years, Iguchi continued to delude himself into believing he could conceal his mistakes. But the charade was about to catch up with him. The separation of duties was making it difficult for him to fabricate the lost funds that were now approaching $1 billion.

By now he had conducted approximately 30,000 unauthorized transactions and was responsible for an average loss of $400,000 per day.[11] A red flag would certainly go up if he continued to make unauthorized trades. Despite every argument he made to convince himself that he could still fix the problem, Iguchi finally caved in.

Without a doubt, he had become the epitome of the Peter Principle. In just over a decade he had risen to his level of incompetence. In July 1995 Iguchi realized he couldn't wait any longer for federal regulators or Daiwa's internal auditors to detect his fraud. As far as he was concerned, they were as incompetent as he was. Although Daiwa's internal auditors had checked out their own New York branch several times since 1984, they never independently confirmed the balance sheets being held a few blocks away at Bankers Trust.

Iguchi had created the problem and now his life was filled with "fear, guilt, and deception." It was time to confess.

Iguchi sat down and began writing. Thirty pages later, he had bared his soul in a rambling, detailed account of when the fraud began and how it was executed. In his epistle, Iguchi told of an audit that failed to notice a $100 million discrepancy and a company practice that neglected to require crosschecking daily trades against monthly summaries.[12]

On July 24 he sent a copy of his "personal and confidential" confession to Daiwa President Akira Fujita.

Like Daiwa's other quixotic policies and procedures, Fujita didn't fire Iguchi for another two months. Perhaps it was because Iguchi hinted that there would be "zero possibility" that anyone would ever detect the loss if Daiwa bought back some of the customer securities he had illegally sold.

Unsure what to do, Fujita called Daiwa directors in Japan and suggested they attend a meeting in New York. On July 28 and 29 Daiwa officials met at the Park Lane Hotel with Mashahiro Tsuda, the general manager of Daiwa's New York office and, surprisingly, Iguchi, to decide how to handle the crisis.

Managing Director Hiroyuki Yamaji had a brainstorm: Iguchi only needed to destroy the disk that held his original confession, then rewrite it and omit all that incriminating evidence about complicity from his superiors. If Iguchi fell on his sword, Yamaji thought, the company would be saved from a potentially embarrassing financial scandal.[13]

They also agreed that silence is golden. If they could stall for time, they could probably unload some real estate and bond holdings and raise enough cash to plug the $1.1 billion hole. Iguchi later claimed that they requested he continue to conceal his losses and forge documents, which he did in order to pay the interest on securities he had taken from custodial accounts.[14]

Weeks later, on August 8, Daiwa felt secure enough to inform Japan's Ministry of Finance of the massive loss. Yamaji shared the secret with banking bureau director Yoshimasa Nishimura who, says Yamaji, agreed that Japan's punch-drunk economy wasn't ready for more bad news. Nishimura later corrected Yamaji's account of the conversation by stating that he had only instructed Daiwa to make a thorough investigation before revealing the scandal. Japan was already paying a premium to borrow in foreign markets and this disclosure would only drive that borrowing rate higher.

Regardless of who knew what and when it happened, Daiwa assumed their $390 billion in assets would help them weather the financial and public relations storms that would surround them.

It didn't.

On September 18, a very long two months after Iguchi made his confession, the Ministry of Finance finally deigned to admit the crime to the Federal Reserve and U.S. Treasury officials in New York and Washington. To the company's surprise, the feds weren't impressed with Daiwa's attempt to cover up the scandal and were furious that Daiwa hadn't informed them earlier.

They began digging into Daiwa's internal policies and realized the bank had conspired to keep the true nature of Iguchi's dual office responsibilities secret as far back as 1993. When regulators inspected Daiwa, they had been shown what appeared to be a storage room. It was only after they left that traders, under the supervision of Iguchi, entered the "storage room" to resume their business day.

They also learned that as recently as July 1995 — just three months earlier — Daiwa claimed to own $600 million in government securities that Iguchi had already sold to cover his losses.[15] Around that same time, Daiwa had also ordered the destruction of 1,500 boxes of documents, accounting books, and receipts. Nothing to do with Iguchi, Daiwa claimed, just routine housekeeping...[16]

Although the company was facing its own judgment day, Iguchi's came first. He was arrested at his home on September 23, and at a later court appearance he pleaded guilty to six counts of fraud, falsifying documents, laundering money, and embezzling $500,000 for his personal use.[17] On October 9 Fujita resigned his post as bank president but remained with Daiwa as a paid adviser.

Then the feds found out that Daiwa still had another surprise up their sleeve. In the following weeks, they discovered the Ministry of Finance had engaged in the conspiracy and maintained a six-week code of silence after learning about Iguchi's $50,000-turned-$1.1 billion mistake.[18]

In November Daiwa's U.S. banking license was revoked. The Federal Reserve gave Daiwa 90 days to pack their bags and get out of the country. The U.S. Attorney's office got in on the act and filed 24 counts of criminal conspiracy and fraud that threatened $1.3 billion in fines.[19]

The following January Daiwa reached an agreement to sell most of its outstanding loans and U.S.-based bank offices to Japanese financial giant, Sumitomo, for roughly $3.37 billion. Sayonara, Daiwa.

Iguchi was sentenced to four years in prison and still faces $2.6 million in fines and restitution for his role in the fraud.

Down but not out, Iguchi followed the lead of rogue trader-turned-author Nick Leeson. From the privacy of his prison cell, Iguchi wrote his tell-all book, *The Confession*, in which he shares the blame with U.S. and Japanese regulators, who he claims conducted only cursory inspections of his trading department.[20]

Regardless of his book's advance and royalties, Iguchi could hardly come close to repaying what he lost.

He'd still be shy about $1.1 billion.

References

[1]Levinson, Marc, and Meyer, Michael, "Billion Dollar Bath," *Newsweek*, Oct. 9, 1995, 54.

[2]Sapsford, Jathon (in Tokyo); Sesit, Michael R. (in London); and O'Brien, Timothy L. (in New York), "How Daiwa Bond Man In New York Cost Bank $1.1 Billion in Losses," *Wall Street Journal*, Sep. 27, 1995, A1.

[3]Greenwald, John, "A Blown Billion," *Time*, Oct. 9, 1995, 60.

[4]O'Brien, Timothy L., and Ono, Yumiko, "U.S. Says Daiwa Bank Officials Conspired," *Wall Street Journal*, Oct. 20, 1995, B13.

[5]Sapsford, Jathon, et al., op. cit., Al.

[6]Ibid.

[7]Sapsford, Jathon, et al., op. cit., A6.

[8]Sapsford, Jathon, "Daiwa Scandal Creates Fallout For Tokyo," *Wall Street Journal*, Sep. 28, 1995, A16.

[9]Sapsford, Jathon, et al., Sep. 27, 1995, A6.

[10]Levinson, Marc, and Meyer, Michael, op. cit., 55.

[11]Ibid.

[12]Shirouzu, Norihiko, "Daiwa Bank's Oversight Is Called Lax In Letter By Trader Who Hid Losses," *Wall Street Journal*, Dec. 12, 1995, A16.

[13]Hirsh, Michael with Levinson, Marc; Lee, Charles S.; Thomas, Rich; and Takayama, Hideko in Tokyo, "After the Deluge," *Newsweek*, Nov. 13, 1995, 57.

[14]O'Brien, Timothy L., and Ono, Yumiko, op. cit., B13.

[15]Ibid.

[16]Staff Reporter, "Daiwa Probe Targets Disposal of Receipts Before News of Losses," *Wall Street Journal*, Nov. 27, 1995, B2.

[17]O'Brien, Timothy L., and Ono, Yumiko, op. cit., B13.

[18]Hirsh, Michael, et al., op. cit, 57.

[19]Hirsh, Michael, et al., op. cit., 56.

[20]Bremner, Brian in Tokyo, "The Daiwa Scandal: Blaming The Regulators," *Business Week*, Jan 20, 1997.

NICHOLAS LEESON
"Rogue Trader"

Barings Bank employee Nick Leeson lived in a modestly furnished luxury apartment in one of Singapore's most exclusive neighborhoods. He had a Porsche in the garage, designer clothes in the closet, and an on-staff maid. But if you had visited on the morning of February 24, 1995, you'd have noticed a few things were missing.

Nick Leeson and more than a billion dollars of the bank's money.

• •

Nicholas Leeson was an average kid. He grew up in a government-subsidized housing project in the London suburb of Watford, where he played soccer and attended Kingsway Junior School. But the son of a working-class plasterer was cast from a different mold and wasn't about to settle for an average life.[1]

He was offered an education at Parmiter's, a school founded in the 18th century by a silk merchant who wanted to see poor but promising boys receive an education. For Leeson, Parmiter would provide the tools he needed to pass school exams and enter prestigious Oxford University. But the plan to attend college fell apart when he failed his final math exam in June 1983.

Armed with only a high school diploma, the 18-year-old gave up on his formal education and took a job as a junior clerk at Coutts & Company, a prestigious private bank. For the teenager raised under modest means, it was a perfect fit.[2] The banking business surrounded him with money, power, and prestige. He enjoyed the work and moved quickly through the ranks.

Then in 1987 the 20-year-old found work as a settlement clerk in Futures & Options at Morgan Stanley & Co. in London. He was now earning $46,000 annually plus a $46,000 yearly bonus. By June 1989, with a sizeable salary to reflect his confidence, he was ready to move on. A corporate headhunter landed him a perfect position in the Settlements Division of Barings plc.

Founded by Francis Baring in 1762, the venerable institution counted Queen Elizabeth II among its depositors and pointed with pride that it had financed the Napoleonic Wars and the Louisiana Purchase. However, they preferred not to discuss the period in 1890 when Barings came close to folding after their Argentinean investments failed. Fortunately, the firm was rescued by the generous Bank of England which provided them with an emergency cash transfusion equivalent to $1.3 billion in today's currency.[3]

By the early 1990s Barings had coasted through decades of low-key successes and steady but otherwise unremarkable growth. Where once they had ventured into new businesses and taken minor risks, the market now was changing and they were working in an arena where more savvy American traders were cleaning up. To them, Leeson represented a new breed of Barings employee: young, sharp, and aggressive. During September and October 1991 he was assigned to an investigative unit where he examined alleged trading discrepancies in the firm's Tokyo office. His work resulted in the dismissal of three employees.[4]

In 1992 Leeson experienced two major events: in March, he married 21-year-old Lisa Sims, a clerk who worked for a Barings stockbroker; the second event took place in April, when they moved to Singapore.[5] Geographically and culturally, the two offices were worlds apart. In London, blue-blooded executives worked with efficiency and a sense of honor. In Singapore, young neocolonialist traders were bolstered by their image as gunslinging financiers. Regardless, the differences wouldn't prevent Barings from its manifest destiny of expanding its trading operations into the much-hyped world market. The firm decided Singapore would be their base and Leeson would be their man in the East. Managing the futures operations of Barings Securities, Ltd. was a major responsibility for the 25-year-old — but to whom was he responsible?

When he arrived, no one knew exactly why he was there or to whom he reported. No matter. As far as Leeson was concerned, life was treating him well. Very well. Just seven years after failing his math exam, he had become one of the rising stars in Singapore's financial community. In the exotic setting of colonial homes, manicured lawns, and cricket grounds in Bukit Timah,

Leeson was viewed as part of the aristocracy. Earning nearly $150,000 a year, Leeson bragged about his bonuses, which amounted to nearly $2 million annually, and his unlimited travel budget. Settling near Singapore's Orchard Road — considered the Rodeo Drive of the Pacific Rim — the Leesons accepted Barings' gracious offer to pick up the $9,000 monthly tab on their luxury three-bedroom apartment.

Back in London, Barings officers considered the monthly payment a pittance compared to the profits being generated by their man in Singapore. By early 1994 Leeson presumably was earning Barings a generous multimillion-dollar return for his acumen with derivatives, a quixotic and volatile product that staid banks such as Barings had previously avoided until the late 1980s.

That's when Christopher Heath, the head of Barings Securities in Tokyo, introduced his superiors to derivatives by pushing their use at the exchange to rake in an endless stream of money. With earnings at nearly $7 million per year, Heath became Britain's highest paid executive.

Meanwhile, the conservative, tradition-bound corporate financiers at Barings Brothers were engaged in a cold war with Barings Securities. With aggressive employees like Heath trading their money halfway around the world, they were soon operating out of their element. Still, Barings Securities was theoretically providing two-thirds of the bank's total profit and the London bankers continued to fund these overseas operations.[6]

Occasionally there were consistent but unheeded pleas from Barings' old guard that derivatives needed to be supervised by a more prudent and cautious sales expert. The prevailing attitude within Barings management, however, was to turn a blind eye as long as derivatives continued to pump cash into the coffers. At the time, this attitude appeared to be logical. By the last half of 1994, Leeson claimed Barings Futures had earned them $30 million, or 20 percent of the firm's overall $157 million profit. If his figures had been honest, proprietary trading would have been outperforming Barings' traditional investment banking.[7]

To be equitable, the lure of quick profits was not exclusive to Barings. Around the world, the concept of "easy money" was eroding the ability of many securities executives to scrutinize high-energy traders. CFOs were reluctant to admit they didn't comprehend the complexity — or risks — of the highly leveraged derivatives. Even in the United States, more than $1.5 trillion in mutual-fund money was flooding the globe, leading investment and fund managers to stop asking basic questions about disclosure, accounting, value, and risk.[8]

Back in Tokyo, Heath was fed up. It wasn't the money he was making from his investments, it was the money he wasn't receiving from the home office. In 1993, after Barings declined to provide him with the capital he requested for his pet derivatives, he quit in frustration. Since four other Barings managers had dropped in and out of Tokyo within three years, a power vacuum was created and Leeson quickly filled the void.

As Barings' top trader acclimated himself to his starring role, he quickly accumulated more power. Leeson's previous experience as a settlement clerk at Morgan Stanley & Co. convinced Barings that he could clear trades. Although it was in violation of Osaka exchange rules and an industry practice which separated duties, Leeson became both trader and manager. This combination of duties allowed him to confirm his own transactions and write his own checks.

Now he was supervising the "back office" — the department designed to keep a leash on unauthorized or risky trades — and the "front office" — the department designed to initiate business and negotiate deals. Soon, he was executing in-house and client orders from several other offices, particularly Tokyo, which made it impossible for supervisors to establish a check and balance system.[9]

With this privilege, eventually Leeson developed a strategy known in gambling circles as "over- and under-betting." His modus operandi involved buying and selling futures contracts pegged to the Nikkei 225, an index of the value of 225 Japanese stocks. Substantial returns would be generated when both Japan's Nikkei stock index rose and Japanese and European interest rates rose.

Leeson realized he was hedging his bets, since interest rates typically drop as stocks rise, and stocks drop as interest rates increase.[10]

On the trading floor, Leeson was aware that he held sway among the other traders. With a stocky build and booming voice, his physical presence overshadowed the smaller Asian traders. When figures suggested it was time to sell, Leeson would lead the charge to push the market higher and, invariably, the locals would follow. In Singapore, Leeson became known as the Nikkei King.

His bravado overshadowed the fact that his trading responsibilities were supposed to be limited to executing trades at his clients' direction, a rule that Leeson broke regularly. Nor did Leeson adhere to the policy that said his trades were to be made on orders he had received from Barings' Tokyo traders who were watching the Nikkei for small price differences on the Osaka and Singapore International Monetary Exchange (SIMEX). Instead, Leeson barreled ahead on his own course.

Outside the pit, however, there were clear signs that all was not well. Since early 1992, warning signals were being sent. An internal fax by James Bax, then head of the Asian regional office, warned that Leeson's lack of accountability could lead to disaster. "We are in danger of setting up a structure which will prove disastrous, in which we could succeed in losing either a lot of money, client goodwill, or both."[11] Two years later, fellow traders approached officials from SIMEX and warned them of Leeson's risky trading practices. An audit was conducted by SIMEX in August 1994, and the exchange warned Barings that Leeson had "excessive" power. Around the same time, an internal audit conducted by Barings itself suggested that while Leeson was a risk, at least he was a profitable one. If Leeson left Barings, his departure would "speed the erosion of Barings Futures' profitability... Without him, Barings Futures would lack a trader with the right combination" of experience, contacts, trading skills, and local knowledge.[12]

How did Barings react? Barings thanked SIMEX for its information and concern and calmly assured them that they were in full control of the situation. In truth, they were not. Leeson was selective about the information he disclosed. He reported his customer trades to a Tokyo office and his proprietary trades to a London office. Only on paper did he report to the head of Barings' Singapore office.

With no one looking over his shoulder, Leeson was in complete control. In essence, he was grading the math exam he had flunked years earlier — and this time he was determined to pass the test.

But as the Nikkei King was supposedly generating huge profits for Barings, auditors overlooked Error Account No. 88888. Inside this portfolio was the truth behind the rise of Nicholas Leeson.

The traders in Singapore were making small mistakes, either buying too much or too little at the wrong price. Their errors were placed in Baring's London-based Error Account No. 99905. Noticing this high volume of minor errors, Gordon Bowser, the manager in charge of all Barings' derivatives settlements, called from England and explained the London system couldn't handle these trivial transactions. He authorized Leeson to create his own error account file in Singapore.

Leeson's secretary suggested that since '8' was a lucky Chinese number, Error Account No. 88888 would be five times as lucky. For two weeks the Singapore team's errors were placed in the file until Bowser called to explain the London system had been updated. From now on, Singapore's mistakes would again be placed in Error Account No. 99905.

By the end of 1994, when Leeson claimed an earned profit of $30 million, he had actually lost $285 million.[13] Why didn't Barings notice this quarter-billion-dollar red flag? Because Leeson made sure the trades remained privileged information.

Although Error Account No. 88888 had been quiet since Bowser requested all mistakes be filed in the London office, Leeson had retained the file on his computer, secured by a secret password. When asked, Leeson would dismiss the account by explaining that it contained massive purchase orders that were requested

— and presumably paid for — by an anonymous hedge-fund client. Convincingly, he assured Barings, *their* investments were safe.[14]

But like a ticking bomb, Error Account No. 88888 was about to explode in their hands.

By January 1995 the bogus account was $320 million in the red. Understanding that he had to rebuild Barings' fortunes, Leeson realized that he could rescue the bank if only he could double his wager and bet again. He had to raise the stakes. Barings had to provide the funds.

Predicting the Nikkei would trade within a narrow range between 19,000 and 21,000,[15] Leeson thought he had a safe bet. He didn't. On January 17 an earthquake measuring 7.5 smashed the city of Kobe, killing 5,000 people and prompting catastrophic aftershocks in the Japanese market. Within a week, the Nikkei index dropped seven percent.[16] Back in Singapore, Leeson had a last shot. He would drive the market up by increasing the number of contracts held by Barings. If other traders followed his lead, he could prompt the market to rebound and stabilize near 19,000.

This time, however, the locals failed to follow his lead.

The massive facade of ignorance that had been erected in London finally began to crumble. On February 8 Barings' London office flew Anthony Hawes, their group treasurer, to Singapore to discuss the company's holdings. Within two weeks, Barings' regional officers requested that Leeson reduce the number of Nikkei contracts.

This time Leeson was unable to hedge his bets. Like a gambler who continually bets on black as the wheel repeatedly lands on red, all he could do was double his bets and try to break even. Obviously, Leeson's plan would have worked if Barings had provided him with unlimited capital. But in the two months leading up to Barings' collapse, the institution had already provided their star trader with $850 million — a sum slightly larger than the firm's entire capital base. Why did Barings go along with this perilous gambit? It may have been blind faith in Leeson or their acceptance of his explanation that his mysterious corporate client would redeposit the funds within days.

In Leeson's mind, he had already accepted the inevitable. On February 15 Leeson's wife called movers and arranged to ship their possessions back to England. Leeson tried to soothe his nerves by taking in a round of golf on an island off Singapore.

On February 23 Leeson purchased another 4,000 contracts in a falling market but he still couldn't stop the market from dropping 300 points. He then turned his attention to his returns and saw that he was firmly in the red by $1.3 billion — give or take a few million. His nerves shot, his capital squandered, the Nikkei King abdicated his throne. He left the trading floor and raced to the bathroom to throw up. After being confronted by two senior officials who asked him about his unusual trades, he left the office around 2 p.m. and never returned.[17]

On February 24 Leeson rented a Mercedes and drove to the exclusive Regent Hotel in Kuala Lumpur, where he brashly charged his room to his Barings corporate credit card. Back in Singapore, SIMEX would be requesting $40 million in margin payments.

On February 25 Leeson spent his birthday whitewater rafting in Borneo. Meanwhile, in Singapore, James Bax was reading a fax sent by Leeson from his hotel. Explaining the details of his risky trades, Leeson ended the note offering his "sincere apologies for the predicament I have left you in."

Barings was near death, but this time the British government wasn't in a forgiving mood. The Bank of England shut off life support and voted to put Barings into bankruptcy.

What followed was a finger pointing exercise of Olympic proportions. The conservative members of Barings Bank blamed the aggressive young traders of Barings Securities, the young traders blamed the conservative members for not guarding Leeson, and the press alternately placed the blame on "risky derivatives," a "rogue trader," or a conspiracy of silence that reached into the upper levels of Barings Brothers & Co.

On March 3 the fugitive financier was arrested as he disembarked from a plane at the Frankfurt airport. Immediately, sympathetic attorneys fought to keep their young charge from being extradited to Singapore. Perhaps their motives were humane. In a place where vandalizing a car can prompt a good caning, no one dared dream of the punishment Leeson would receive for bankrupting a centuries-old institution.

For nine months Leeson engaged in legal gymnastics to return to England. In media interviews, the master trader became the master of the understatement. During an interview with David Frost, Leeson calmly explained that he had simply "lost" the money, not stolen it, and added, "Taking a futures position is a 50/50 gamble. And the laws of probability had to say that I would win some. Unfortunately, I lost more than I won."

Eventually, Leeson also lost his fight against being extradited and was returned to Singapore. He was held in the medium security Tanah Merah Prison until he was ushered into the courtroom to listen as more than 11 charges of forgery and cheating were read aloud. When it was all over, Leeson pleaded guilty and received six-and-a-half years on two counts of fraud. Fearing he could have received 84 years, the relatively light sentence may have been the result of the best trade Leeson ever made. He cooperated with the prosecution and admitted that during his efforts to conceal his losses, some of his superiors may have known about his ruse.

As the dust settled, Leeson apologists explained that the 28-year-old meant well, but since he received the support of a system that rewarded profits at the expense of responsibility, he gradually came to believe his own myth. Having never posted significant losses or suffered through a bear market, they explained, Leeson didn't know what to do when the time came to cut his losses and rebuild.

Senior management, who had at least three years worth of warnings, were also absolved of their responsibilities by those who claim that the deregulation of Britain's financial sector had left them in the lurch. Suddenly facing formidable competition from Japanese and American investors, they had to enter markets with which they were unfamiliar. The change in investing prompted them to troll the waters for savvy young traders and Leeson was snagged. Although they should have thrown this catch back, they didn't. The corporate culture at Barings wanted to generate disproportionately huge profits from a tiny capital base. Likewise, Leeson wanted to please his bosses and increase his own economic and social standing.

It was a fatal attraction.

For three years, Leeson eluded six layers of regulation. No one at Barings, its auditor Coopers & Lybrand, the Bank of England, the London securities regulator, the Singapore authorities, or the two exchanges had a complete picture — or admitted to knowing — what Leeson was up to.

As far as the government of Singapore and the Bank of England were concerned, the ultimate blame lay at the feet of six top Barings executives and four outside directors who chose not to educate themselves on the risk of derivatives. Reports from both parties criticized Barings officials for institutional incompetence and a total failure of internal controls, claiming some Barings executives were either grossly negligent or willfully blind to the truth. Barings officials, they suggested, were too scared to face the truth. If they had stopped to check the math and realized Leeson was merely building paper profits, Barings' global expansion would have been hindered and it was feared there may not have been enough funds available to cover annual bonuses.

Ironically, the lack of internal controls didn't hurt everyone. Within weeks of Barings' collapse, the Dutch banking firm Internationale Nederlanden Groep picked through the rubble and agreed to buy Barings.[18]

The cost?

One pound sterling. Roughly $2.30.

What a steal.

References

[1]Fisher, Jennifer, "The Bloke Who Broke The Bank," *U.S. News & World Report*, Mar. 13, 1995, 70.

[2]Dalglish, Brenda, and Wallace, Bruce, "Breaking The Bank," *Maclean's*, Mar. 13, 1995, 47.

[3]Dalglish, Brenda, and Wallace, Bruce, op. cit., 46.

[4]Fisher, Jennifer, op. cit., 70.

[5]Ibid.

[6]Chua-Eoan, Howard G. with Colmey, John; Gibney, Frunk Jr.; Desmond, Edward W.; Branegan, Jay; Hillenbrand, Barry; van Voorst, Bruce; and Subramanian, Sribala, "Going For Broke," *Time*, Mar. 13, 1995, 42.

[7]Powell, Bill with Pedersen, Daniel; Underhill, William; Levinson, Marc; Clifton, Tony; Roberts, Melissa; Strasser, Steven; and McKillop, Peter, "Busted," *Newsweek*, Mar. 13, 1995, 42.

[8]Dwyer, Paula with Glasgall, William; Foust, Dean; and Burns, Greg, "The Lesson From Barings' Straits," *Business Week*, Mar. 13, 1995, 30.

[9]Wallace, Bruce, "Cultural Differences," *Maclean's*, Mar. 20, 1995, 33.

[10]Powell, Bill, et al., op. cit., 40.

[11]Chua-Eoan, et al., op. cit., 46.

[12]Ibid.

[13]Dwyer, Paula, "The Singapore Slinger: A Cautionary Tale," *Business Week*, Jan. 15, 1996, 16.

[14]Chua-Eoan, et al., op. cit., 45.

[15]Ibid.

[16]Ibid.

[17]Dwyer, Paula, op. cit., 16.

[18]Wallace, Bruce, op. cit., 32.

ROBERT CITRON
"Who Do You Trust?"

In the gray world of bureaucracy, Robert Citron was about as gray as they come. Exactly the sort of low-key, Walter Mitty-type functionary whom the voters of Orange County, California, repeatedly chose to reelect as treasurer. Frugal and nondescript, he was the sort of man they could trust with their money.

Or could they?

•••

Sixty-nine-year-old Robert L. Citron was not a flashy politician. You wouldn't see him glad-handing potential campaign contributors, kissing babies, or working himself into a sweat while delivering a rousing stump speech. But after 24 years as treasurer of Orange County, California, by 1994 Citron had built up a power base that any politician would envy.

Perhaps it was his mild manner that intrigued voters. Picture a quiet candidate who shuns fancy offices, expensive suits, and elaborate fund-raising dinners. A politico who lived in a bland house, worked in a bland office, and was thrilled to do the same bland job. Citron led such a Spartan existence, voters thought, he would clearly invest county funds as if they were his own: prudently, cautiously, and carefully.

So if anyone had a fleeting thought of scrutinizing Citron, it was quickly dismissed. He was doing right by them. Other county governments should be so lucky. While their treasurers were generating a soft five percent return on their money, Citron was pumping out annual returns of around nine percent.[1]

Sure, Citron could have played it safe like everyone else, but by the mid-1980s local governments were no longer content — or able to survive — on the sort of chump change a five percent return afforded. Municipal fund managers like Citron were given their orders by county commissions: find new ways to make the money we need to operate.

Citron didn't have to travel very far to find the road to riches. In 1985 he received authorization from the Orange County Board of Supervisors to invest in reverse repurchase agreements.[2] Using securities as collateral, Citron's investment pool received loans to purchase additional securities. The old school investor was seduced by this new method of doing business.

All the treasurer had to do was borrow "expensive" money and repay the loan later using "cheaper" money or the appreciation earned on his securities.

It was such a simple concept that within a decade, his investment pool had acquired nearly $21 billion in assets, owed slightly over $13 billion in debt, and boasted a book value of just over $7 billion.

He continued to invest the county's money in interest-sensitive derivatives contracts, and as long as interest rates kept going down, Citron's investments kept going up. Why the ultraconservative Orange County Commission allowed the treasurer to make astronomical wagers on a 50/50 prospect is anybody's guess, but they did. Perhaps no one wanted to believe that behind his Casper Milquetoast demeanor, Citron was viewed by other county treasurers as an aggressive trader who enjoyed "pushing the envelope."[3]

In early 1994, however, a red flag was raised. Costa Mesa CPA John Moorlach (R), faced Citron (D) in a race for the treasurer's office. During his campaign, Citron defended his dependency on derivatives. "We do have a different strategy from most counties," he said, "but we are aggressive within prudent limits."[4] He added that despite the vast number of his derivative investments, "We don't use any exotic stuff."[5]

After Moorlach pressed Citron to make his investment portfolio public (something Citron had traditionally refused to do), Citron provided a list of securities held in the county investment pool. After scrutinizing the data, Moorlach was shocked: there was not enough information to determine the investments' value, risk, or even what they were. Moorlach alerted voters, telling them the "listing is junk," and added that with derivatives, "When you win, you win big. When you lose, you can also lose big."[6]

What did Moorlach receive for his concern? A decisive defeat. And why not? Everyone was happy with the status quo.

Thanks to Citron's golden touch, the county's investments the previous year earned $170 million compared to the meager $117 million in property taxes they had earned. The generous profits the county had grown accustomed to clouded nearly everyone's judgement.[7] Instead of explaining his investments in monthly or quarterly reports, Citron was only required to present his fatted calf to the county annually. He did so by showing profits, trumpeting his achievements, and taking credit for a robust economy.

This annual celebration of profits was fine with county commissioners. They could still announce in campaign brochures that they were instrumental in making Orange County the wealthiest in the state. Voters were happy to receive improved municipal services and looked forward to a new $82 million police, fire, and emergency communication system as well as a new stadium for their beloved Los Angeles Rams. Disneyland was making arrangements to spend the $750 million in county funds they'd receive to assist with their planned $3 billion expansion.[8]

But in late 1994, interest rates reversed their downward trend and began to climb. Suddenly Orange County wasn't the happiest place on earth anymore.

The novice investor tried to make up for early losses by pouring more money into derivatives. As rates continued to spiral upward, nearly $8 billion in structured securities left him paying more on what he had borrowed than what he was earning through his investments. Citron had become a downhill racer and the slope was getting steeper.

It must have been a shock for the old financial functionary. Although he may have wanted to play it safe, the damn state and the damn commissioners couldn't manage their money, and he was forced to be greedy and take some risks...

On December 1 the county commissioners admitted that due to the increase in interest rates, its $7.4 billion investments in derivatives and reverse repos had lost $1.5 billion. At an emergency meeting, supervisors began discussing the dreaded 'B' word: bankruptcy. Lenders were smelling blood.

First Boston Corporation demanded a $200 million payment on $2.6 billion in reverse repurchase agreements.[9] When First Boston couldn't squeeze a payment out of Orange County, they responded by liquidating their entire holdings of Orange County collateral. As Morgan Stanley, Merrill Lynch, Nomura Securities International, and others prepared to sell off their own investments, Orange County beat them to the punch.

The county safeguarded what remained of their fund by filing Chapter 9 to protect themselves from bankruptcy. In an instant, the stadium, the emergency system, and the new Disneyland parking lots were on hold. Government workers wondered about their pensions and county officials scrambled to think of ways to save their skins...

If we spread the debt evenly over Orange County residents, they thought, that'd only be $2,500 per household... Maybe we should raise taxes? Not a chance. Nobody wants higher taxes. Cutting corners should be the first order of business. Do teachers really need a raise? Garbage didn't *have* to be picked up that often, did it? Why wait until June to close the schools? Perhaps the first thing we should do is get rid of that investment pool...

On December 4 Citron resigned his post, which was filled by his second-in-command, CPA Matthew Raabe. Citron left behind a paltry $100,339-a-year salary and a massive $1.7 billion sea of red ink.[10] Soon ripples the size of tidal waves rushed over U.S. markets. The following day the $1.2 trillion municipal bond market dropped a full point. That same day Texas acknowledged losses of $70 million from repurchase agreements and reverse repos in a state investment pool. Standard & Poor's downgraded Orange County's bonds from AA- to D, which added millions to the costs of borrowing — if in fact there was anyone willing to loan Orange County a dime.

By filing Chapter 9 they had gained some breathing room. Orange County officials began to look for the fall guy. Who cares if Citron wasn't lining his own pockets with the investment returns? Someone had to pay.

But if the officials had looked in a mirror, they may have recognized the guilty parties. Like the Barings executives who watched idly as Nicholas Leeson showered them with paper profits and drained off their capital, the Orange County officials reacted to Citron's investment strategies with a policy of hear no evil, see no evil, speak no evil. Why should they rock the boat when they were receiving an endless flow of cash and the bragging rights of being one of the nation's richest counties?

By now, however, they were on the rocks and they weren't about to take the fall for this arrogant, ignorant, incompetent county treasurer. In April 1995, at Citron's day of reckoning, no one rushed to his defense as the mild-mannered treasurer admitted he made false statements to investors and diverted $107 million in interest from an investment pool to the county's coffers. He pleaded guilty to six felony counts of securities fraud and mismanagement of county funds.[11]

Facing 14 years in prison and a $10 million fine,[12] Citron had to come up with a way out. He began a campaign to generate sympathy for himself like he had once generated millions for the county. He began by placing the blame squarely on Raabe's shoulders. Citron claimed that as a CPA, his deputy understood these types of investments better than he did.

Then, adopting the persona of a naive senior citizen who had fallen for a scam artist, he pointed the finger at a Merrill Lynch investment counselor who had "talked him into" the risky investments and arranged loans to the county amounting to more than $1 billion.

In the courtroom, Citron's attorney portrayed his client as a frail, brain-damaged man who struggled to analyze data (a portrayal voters had never seen in Citron's campaign literature). This time Citron's gamble worked. He was sentenced to just one year in the county jail, a $100,000 fine, five years' probation, and 1,000 hours of community service. (The jail sentence was later reduced to days in jail and evenings at home.)[13]

Orange County realized this was an opportunity to regain some of their money and jumped on the "brain-damaged" treasurer bandwagon. Arguing Citron was duped by Merrill Lynch who had recommended the derivative investments, the county filed a $2 billion civil suit. Since Citron had exceeded his authority to make the investments, they claimed, the transactions were invalid and Merrill Lynch should return to the county all collateral and interest.

The plan had merit. In 1984 the city of San Jose had sued Merrill Lynch and other brokerage firms for $60 million in investment losses. To avoid litigation, Merrill Lynch kicked in $750,000.[14] But in October 1995, Federal Judge John Ryan of the U.S. Bankruptcy Court saw it differently. He threw out Orange County's lawsuit and told county attorneys they needed better legal grounds for suing the brokerage firm.

As the lawsuit was dragging through the courts, county administrators were patiently explaining to voters that a half-cent sales tax increase would be the only way to deal with the crisis. Wary of believing the same officials who helped take them on a $1.7 billion ride, voters rejected the proposal by a 3-2 margin. With the tax hike rejected, deep spending cuts were put in place.

Orange County cut or laid off employees from more than 2,800 positions, or 16 percent of its workforce. The general operating budget (the part actually controlled by the county) was slashed by roughly 41 percent to $188 million. But when it came to spending their total $3.7 billion budget, the county's hands were tied. Since about 90 percent of this money came from state and federal funds, the county had to adhere to nearly 50 rules, regulations, and restrictions established by state and federal guidelines.[15]

The meltdown received attention far beyond the mansions of Orange County. On Wall Street and Capitol Hill, Securities & Exchange Commission officials and congressmen beat the "watchdog" drum and proposed new methods of guarding municipal funds and investors who deal in derivatives. Unlike pension fund managers who have to price their holdings each day, they argued, municipalities could lose money 24-hours-a-day as the treasurer patiently — and dangerously — waited for the market to turn their way. Meanwhile, back in Orange County, Huntington Beach Treasurer Donald L. Watson suggested the county treasurer be required to provide quarterly reports, which didn't seem like such a bad idea anymore.[16]

By the spring of 1997, Citron was still trying to distance himself from his role in the collapse. At the trial of Matthew Raabe, who was on trial for the same charges that had landed Citron in jail, the ex-treasurer testified that his former assistant had "talked him into" skimming nearly $90 million in interest earnings and placing it in a treasury account for the county's benefit.

When asked why he approved the diversion, Citron explained, "I trusted Mr. Raabe. He was a certified public accountant."

Raabe's attorneys, however, stated that he was only following his boss's orders. Raabe was convicted.

Not everyone was handed a setback by the Orange County debacle, however.

In March 1995 John Moorlach did what none of Citron's opponents had been able to do in nearly a quarter of a century. The certified public accountant who warned of Citron's risky business long before it became public knowledge was finally named treasurer of Orange County.

References

[1]Byrnes, Nanette, "With Returns Like These, Why Ask Questions?" *Business Week*, Dec. 19, 1994, 30.

[2]Gottschalk Jr., Earl C., "Derivatives Roil California Political Race," *Wall Street Journal*, Apr. 15, 1994, C1.

[3]Byrnes, Nanette op. cit., 30.

[4]Gottschalk Jr., Earl C., op. cit., Cl.

[5]Gottschalk Jr., Earl C., op. cit., C22.

[6]Gottschalk Jr., Earl C., op. cit., Cl.

[7]Byrnes, Nanette, "Orange County Is Looking Green Around The Gills," *Business Week*, Dec. 26, 1994, 66.

[8]Ibid.

[9]Spiro, Leah Nathans with Byrnes, Nanette, and Schiller, Zachary, "Today, Orange County..." *Business Week*, Dec. 19, 1994, 28.

[10]Byrnes, Nanette, op. cit., 30.

[11]Staff Reporter, "Crime And Punishment," *Investors Business Daily*, Nov. 21, 1996.

[12]Orwall, Bruce, "Citron, Ex-Treasurer of Orange County, Gets Year in Jail for Role in Bankruptcy," *Wall Street Journal*, Nov. 20, 1996, B8.

[13]Ibid.

[14]Byrnes, Nanette with Spiro, Leah Nathans, "Will Merrill Take A Hit in Orange County?" *Business Week*, Feb. 13, 1995, 86.

[15]Oliver, Charles, "One Year Later, How Has Orange County Fared?" *Investors Business Daily*, May 30, 1996.

[16]Byrnes, Nanette, op. cit., 30.

PRUDENTIAL-BACHE
"Solid as a Rock?"

In 1982 the Bache Group was just a struggling securities company with an uninspiring track record and an uninspired staff. Then a new company took over and a new boss arrived — a savior who shook up the old order and soon rechristened the flagging firm. With its new name, Prudential-Bache, the firm grew stronger based on the goodwill of the century-old insurance giant. But in the process, it lost the trust and much of the savings of 400,000 investors by using a fatal combination of suspect investments and false advertising. The resulting financial black eye became as big as the Rock of Gibraltar.

• •

If you had walked into the New York headquarters of the Bache Group in the summer of 1982, you would have noticed a distinct sense of mediocrity. For a company supposedly selling financial security, the promise of wealth was nowhere to be seen. There was nothing dynamic about the company... its furnishings, the signage, the lobby, or the attitudes of the employees. But all that was about to change.

A year earlier, Prudential Insurance Company had purchased Bache as a subsidiary to sell stocks and bonds to its 12 million policyholders, a move that was sure to inject life into the otherwise dormant company.[1] George Ball, fresh from a successful run as president at rival stock brokerage firm E.F. Hutton, would lead the charge.

It seemed to be a perfect match. Bache needed leadership and Ball loved to lead. The day after his arrival in August 1982 he began shaking the company all the way up to its rafters. The generic lobby was spruced up with new signs and fresh flowers. As the days passed, complimentary pastries and coffee appeared for employees and visitors; female employees were presented with floral bouquets; and at one memorable meeting, Ball surprised the executives by marching them to a neighboring haberdashery to be fitted for new suits. The company, of course, graciously picked up the tab.[2]

Ball's good cheer wasn't extended to every member of the Bache family, however. Within weeks he removed one of Bache's two board directors, fired five senior executives along with 15 of their assistants, and dismissed nearly every member of the executive committee. Where there was dead weight, Ball would sink it. If executives were not up to speed, Ball showed them the door.[3] He cleaned house and made it known that this firm would no longer tolerate second-raters. Ball envisioned the most vibrant and vital securities firm the city had ever seen.

The "clear cutting" he had exercised now required replacements. As Ball had done at Hutton, he put the word out that new brokers were wanted. In exchange for their complete devotion to the company, he promised generous up-front bonuses and commissions. The catch? The "bonus" was actually a temporary loan to be forgiven only after the employee had been with the company for two to three years. In other words, if you didn't cut the mustard, the loan would have to be repaid. Semantics didn't seem to matter to more than 1,000 brokers who flooded the firm.[4]

Now staffed with loyal employees, Ball looked at his new company and saw that Bache's tax shelter division, which was headed up by another high-energy employee, Jim Darr, was ready for a profitable change. Realizing that only wealthy clients concentrated on Bache's tax shelter services, Ball sensed that he could attract a newer market by introducing ways for smaller clients to earn investment income.

With a twist on words, Ball dropped the familiar title 'Tax Investment Department' in favor of the broader term 'Direct Investment Group.' Theoretically, Bache could introduce limited partnerships that would allow small investors to buy a share of the profits from such investment opportunities as oil wells, real estate, and energy exploration. Bache would select the partners, organize the deal, and manage the accounts for an established fee and percentage of capital gains and income.[5]

While this was good news for smaller investors, it was outstanding news for the brokers with whom Ball promised to "share the wealth." Along with Bache and their handpicked co-general partners, brokers who sold investors $25,000 in limited partnerships would receive a commission plus half of the cash the firm received.[6]

Already excited by their up-front bonuses, brokers didn't see this new company policy as a cash cow — this was the entire herd. For this kind of commission, brokers began honing their limited partnership pitches to a razor's edge. But what if the elderly clients who couldn't afford the risk didn't want to invest? Were brokers concerned about the aging clients? Did they display integrity or a lack of compassion? Truth is, many didn't even want to think about it. They were convinced that limited partnerships were good. Good for everyone. Period.

With largesse, Ball cleverly decided that a portion of the remaining profits would not go back into the firm. Instead, they would be distributed to certain executives within the tax shelter department. If any cash was left over, then the co-general partner would receive the rest.[7] Of course, not many companies would be willing to surrender such a large share of their proceeds with just the Bache name selling their services. The chance for a significant return was pretty thin.

A few days later, their chances improved considerably when Ball announced the firm would henceforth be known as Prudential-Bache. The beauty of the name change was that under this new title, clients would now be getting "A Piece of the Rock" with every investment.

Prudential-Bache hit the ground running. Granted unrestricted latitude by Ball, Darr set the tone for the new company by making a Texas developer a co-general partner. This same developer also happened to be a major shareholder in an Arkansas bank. Coincidentally, when Darr wanted to buy a home in Connecticut, he received a $2.1 million loan from the Arkansas bank. Clifton Harrison, another Texas developer whom Darr brought to the attention of Prudential-Bache investors, had pleaded guilty to a felony count of embezzlement in 1967.[8]

But who would have suspected anything was wrong? Although Bache was seen as the runt of the litter, Prudential had a long and distinguished pedigree. Since it began as the Widows & Orphans Friendly Society in 1875, Prudential had been building goodwill for more than a century.[9] In the 1930s, as Depression-era homeowners were struggling to make ends meet, Prudential eased or suspended mortgage payments. It was this kind of altruism that had helped Prudential become the largest insurer in America. Its distribution system included 20,000 insurance agents and financial planners, 6,000 securities brokers, and millions of customers. It was this rock solid reputation that investors depended on and brokers were anxious to be associated with. But the merger would bring with it a flood of problems.

Already involved in life insurance, property and casualty insurance, health care, securities brokerage, and banking, now Prudential was involved in asset management. The new corporate dynamic foreshadowed the fatal attraction between GE and Kidder-Peabody. But at Prudential-Bache, the danger wasn't in the actions of a single "rogue trader," but in a criminal mindset that would sweep through the entire corporation.

The promise of financial rewards increased the motivation of brokers — but now it was motivation by greed rather than customer service. With an eye on extracting commissions from investors, the nebulous and completely meaningless title "financial planner" was used interchangeably with the title "broker." Despite the new corporate spin which stressed the value of integrity ("The most important thing we can earn is your trust," read the ads), sales brochures, videos, and brokers' spiels handed customers deceptive half-truths and overestimations with regard to returns on their investments. In the executive boardrooms, management could only see that profits were resurrecting the once stagnant firm.

Over the following decade, more than 700 partners hooked up with Prudential-Bache, ready to get "A Piece of the Rock" and the money hidden beneath it.[10]

One co-general partner was Graham Resources, which sent a team of executives to explain their product (in this case, the Prudential-Bache Energy Income Fund) to naive brokers. Since the product was clearly foreign to this audience, Graham execs stripped away the complexities of the operation and described the fund in layman's terms. They hoped the brokers would absorb the information so it could be relayed to Prudential-Bache investors. But it didn't really matter. Following the presentation, the Graham reps were surrounded by brokers demanding that the fund be clarified even further (i.e., how much commission was in it for them?).[11]

Attempts to explain the product in truthful terms fell by the wayside. A sales video oversimplified the Energy Income Fund, stating that gas and oil were being sold at distressed prices and smart investors would clean up once prices shot up again. The investment, said the video's spokesman, was projected to give investors "high cash flow, appreciation, and low risk," and a return of "16 to 19 percent."[12]

Within months, the pie-in-the-sky sales pitch had been used to sell nearly $27 million in risky ventures. In total, the firm would eventually rake in $1.3 billion, but by 1992 the battered partnership units would sell for 10 cents to 60 cents on the dollar.[13]

At Prudential-Bache at least, the trickle-down theory of the Reagan era had become a poisonous waterfall. With unspoken approval from executives in New York, hundreds of brokers across the country began finding ways to sell risky investments under the protective umbrella of Prudential's good name.

In Dallas, customers' names were forged on purchase orders, unauthorized trades were hidden by shuffling them between accounts, and, in a most memorable case, a broker conducted trades for a customer who had died five years earlier.[14]

Brokers got rich from commissions on investments sold to wealthy investors and managers got richer thanks to the increased income at their branches. Normally that wouldn't be a problem, but in Dallas, brokers were willing to offer questionable advice to investors who often put an equal amount of their trust and their savings into Prudential-Bache recommended accounts.

One case involved an 84-year-old man who cashed out $400,000 in blue chip stocks to buy junk bonds from a Prudential fund — a move that gave his broker two sizeable commissions. But the broker wasn't satisfied until his client borrowed an additional $100,000 to purchase more junk bonds. The investor eventually lost $128,000.[15]

In the middle to late 1980s, Dallas broker Richard Pascuzzi earned $1 million a year in commissions alone. It was relatively easy considering his modus operandi. In the case of a female client, Pascuzzi acted as her "financial advisor." Over the course of a year, he supervised the purchase and sale of a single stock 25 times and her portfolio eventually racked up a total of 175 transactions. Naturally, the elderly widow was surprised to learn the unauthorized trades were in Prudential-Bache limited partnerships rather than the mutual funds she had requested.[16]

Pascuzzi's work ethic wasn't lost on a coworker. Manager Charles Grose wrote a memo to Regional Director R. Peter Archbold advising him that Pascuzzi's rapid buying and selling of securities reflected "serious irregularities." Archbold responded by advising Grose that Pascuzzi was "a good person" and there would be no action taken. Instead, Pascuzzi continued to receive bigger commissions and company awards, and was named to the Chairman's Council to show he was one of Prudential-Bache's top 90 brokers.[17]

Of course, everything's big in Texas and the internal pilferage grew even bigger when it reached the desk of J. Frederic Storaska, the head of Prudential-Bache spin-off Corporate Executive Services (C.E.S.). Granted virtual autonomy within Prudential-Bache headquarters, Storaska was given private offices designed to impress his entrepreneurial clients.[18]

Prudential-Bache also provided Storaska's department with a corporate jet, a limousine, and a private staff. Personally, Storaska benefited from approximately $5 million in commissions annually and a lifestyle afforded by millions of dollars in unauthorized trades and interest-free loans borrowed from the commission account.[19]

It was a very different lifestyle for the man who began his professional career as a rape crisis counselor. After becoming an E.F. Hutton stockbroker in 1977, Storaska worked with George Ball, the current CEO of Prudential-Bache. After Ball recruited Storaska in 1984, his protege went to work. He catered to millionaire entrepreneurs, showering them with gifts and impressing them with the company limousine and corporate jet.[20]

But for all the wealth he flaunted, Storaska was suspiciously inclined to pad his accounts. At the end of the month, he would invest millions of dollars to pump up his commissions — regardless of whether an investor had actually authorized the purchase. If a customer complained, a "trading error" was declared and Storaska would shuffle the purchase into a different account and successfully hide the owner's identity. This proved helpful in avoiding regulators and reporting rules, and it still gave Storaska a commission on the original sale.

But as in the case of Pascuzzi, there was someone watching: Charles Grose. In 1987 Grose fired off a note to the high-flying trader. "It is unacceptable for any reason for you to place a trade in a customer's account that you have not previously discussed," he wrote. "These are major breaches of internal policies and regulatory rules."[21]

Like the warning shot he fired at Pascuzzi, this memo missed the target. Grose had another chance the following year when he dashed off another warning letter regarding Storaska to Annuities Manager Bob Mitchell in Prudential-Bache's New York office. "There should be no question in your mind that Fred is screwing around...," stressed Grose. "(If you) don't assist me in trying to control Fred, Fred will eventually destroy us both," he said.[22]

Once again, the warning was ignored. Instead, the following month executives discussed ways to increase Storaska's salary and expense account to keep him from joining another company.[23]

By 1990 Prudential was receiving regular warnings of Storaska's trades, but when auditors went to investigate, they were told to back off unless they had Storaska "dead to rights."[24]

For a decade, it seems, management didn't mind as long as half-truths could net full profits. Prudential raked in approximately $8 billion through the limited partnerships.[25]

But you can't fool all of the investors all of the time.

The first crack in the case came in 1989 when Prudential-Bache's suspicious sales practices prompted the first of approximately 250 lawsuits. Some brokers responded by following the lead of other criminal suspects and began shredding internal marketing and training documents — a practice Prudential later explained was in violation of company policy. It was also against the law.

By now, state attorneys general and investors weren't the only ones who contemplated suing. Some bold brokers who feigned surprise at the duplicity of their sales practices filed lawsuits against Prudential-Bache, blaming them for not providing an adequate understanding of their job responsibilities.

Over the next several years, Prudential-Bache lost a total of $1.4 billion, roughly equal to the amount Prudential Insurance paid out to victims of Hurricane Andrew.

Also consider that about 40 percent of Prudential's customers owned limited partnerships in the 1980s, but by 1991 that total had fallen to 12 percent.[26] The dismal track record was enough proof for the executives at Prudential to force Ball out in February 1991.

It may have been the end of an error, but it was the beginning of a long recovery for a once-trusted institution.

*If there is a bright side to the double-dealings of Prudential-Bache, it is the controls put into place following the scandals. In October 1993 Prudential agreed to pay at least $330 million to customers who had been ripped off and another $41 million in fines.[27] What's more, in full-page newspaper ads, the new CEO apologized for Prudential-Bache's "intolerable" behavior. He also dissolved more than $1.4 billion in nonstrategic businesses, fired hundreds of agents and managers, and improved internal controls. Only time will tell if the scandal permanently rocked the Rock.

References

[1]Levinson, Marc, "Investing: Prudential's 400,000 Apologies," *Newsweek*, Nov. 1, 1993, 48.

[2]Keenan, William Jr., "The Prudential Scandal Provides The Ultimate Example Of A Sales Culture Gone Bad," Excerpt From 'Serpent On The Rock', Includes Interview With Author Kurt Eichenwald, *Sales & Marketing Management Magazine*, Sept. 1995, 85.

[3]Ibid.

[4]Keenan, William Jr., op. cit., 86.

[5]Ibid.

[6]Ibid.

[7]Ibid.

[8]Hawkins, Chuck, and Spiro, Leah Nathan, "The Mess At Pru-Bache," *Business Week*, Mar. 4, 1991, 68.

[9]Pard, Terence P., "Scandal Isn't All That Ails The Pru," *Fortune*, March 21, 1994, 53.

[10]Fallon, Kathryn Jackson; McCarroll, Thomas; and Zagorin, Adwn, "Socking The Rock," *Time*, Nov. 1, 1993, 57.

[11]Keenan, William Jr., op. cit., 89.

[12]Ibid.

[13]Hawkins, Chuck op. cit., 69.

[14]Eichenwald, Kurt, "Fat Commissions And Scarce Profits: Except From 'Misplaced Trust – A Tale Of Texas Brokers'," *New York Times*, May, 24, 1993, D1.

[15]Eichenwald, Kurt, op. cit., D8.

[16]Ibid.

[17]Ibid.

[18]Eichenwald, Kurt, "Prudential's Firm Within A Firm: Except From 'Misplaced Trust - A Tale Of Texas Brokers'," *New York Times*, May, 25, 1993, D1.

[19]Ibid.

[20]Ibid.

[21]Ibid.

[22]Ibid.

[23]Ibid.

[24]Ibid.

[25]Schroeder, Michael, and Spiro, Leah Nathan, "Is Prudential Playing Hardball?," *Business Week*, Nov. 15, 1993, 159.

[26]Spiro, Leah Nathan, and Hawkins, Chuck, "Pru Secutities: What The Scandal May Cost," *Business Week*, July 5, 1993, 88.

[27]Fallon, Kathryn Jackson, op. cit., 57.

CHARLES KEATING
(a.k.a. "Mr. Cheating")

"I'm going to write my congressman!"

It's a threat generally expressed by average citizens in a last-ditch effort to correct an injustice. Sadly, solitary letters don't often carry much weight. Rather, the laws of economics suggest complaints to politicians accompanied by generous campaign contributions stand a stronger chance of being heard.

Buying the muscle of five congressmen kept financier Charles Keating in business for an additional two years — just long enough to cost the taxpayers an extra couple of billion dollars.

• •

As the economy of the late 1970s was pummeled by rampant inflation, investors pulled their money out of savings and loans (S&Ls) and headed for more lucrative pastures. Eventually, the situation became so dire that S&Ls requested permission from the federal government to expand their investment pool.

When the Carter administration gave its blessings, the conservative S&Ls were no longer restricted to simple home loans. With their newfound freedom, the thrifts shifted gears and entered into real estate, resort development opportunities, and junk bond investments. To their dismay, they continued to lose depositors.

Then in 1980 things begin to change. During a midnight meeting in Washington, D.C., congressmen struck a deal to lure wandering depositors back to the ailing thrifts: they increased the amount of federally insured deposits from $40,000 to $100,000.[1] That did it. Soon, billions of dollars were heading back into the S&Ls and the money train was picking up speed.[2]

Two years later, a bill sponsored by Senator Jake Garn (R-UT) and Representative Fernand St. Germain (D-RI) further eased restrictions. Now hundreds of S&Ls could enter into riskier in-vestments such as speculative land development projects. Cyn-ics might consider this merely a payback by St. Germain who may have felt indebted to the U.S. League of Savings Institutions. One of their lobbyists had allowed the congressman to run up a $20,000 bar and restaurant tab on his account.[3]

In hindsight, the Garn-St. Germain Act may not have been necessary. As a matter of fact, it proved to be dangerous. S&Ls began attracting new get-rich-quick bankers whose only problem was figuring out how to spend their depositors' money. A few bank executives decided to invest in extravagant personal sala-ries and corporate jets, while others found it advantageous to fund political junkets at exotic resorts.[4]

As bankers tried desperately to out-greed one another, they were minor leaguers compared to Charles Keating, the high-roll-ing Californian whose previous claim to fame had been his cru-sade against porn publisher Larry Flynt. In 1984, Keating, the chairman of American Continental Corporation (ACC), a residen-tial construction company, set his sights on and secured Lincoln Savings and Loan of Phoenix. For a homebuilder, this was a dream come true. Not only would he be able to expand his empire into Arizona, Keating would now have the key to the bank and plenty of capital to back up his deals.[5]

But there was one nagging problem...

Regulators from the San Francisco office of the Federal Home Loan Bank Board (FHLBB) were checking out suspicious prac-tices at dozens of S&Ls. As they began digging through Lincoln's paperwork, they found sizeable loans being made without ap-praisals and credit checks. Also, Lincoln's loan officers had been replaced by employees of ACC who had little — if any — banking experience. Regulators also discovered Lincoln Savings was break-ing the equity rule which restricted direct investments from S&Ls to a safe 10 percent of its assets.

To Keating, who was determined to cash in on lax regula-tions, restrictions like this were born to be flaunted.

In 1986 he protested the ruling in two ways: he ignored it by overspending the 10 percent limit by $600 million;[6] then he had future Federal Reserve Board Chairman Alan Greenspan write a letter stating that Lincoln Savings was "a financially strong institution that presents no foreseeable risk."[7] The letter had no affect on anyone within the FHLBB and the investigation continued. Undaunted, Keating had other tricks up his sleeve: he created multiple subsidiaries that made it impossible to trace where the money was going; then he covered his tracks by backdating documents to throw off regulators.

Witnessing the impending disaster was Edwin J. Gray, a Reagan appointee who was then serving as chairman of the FHLBB. Unfortunately, Gray and other regulators were too busy controlling the damage of other self-destructing thrifts to give Keating their undivided attention.

Still, the banker was annoyed by the looming threat of government interference and a possible takeover. If he was going to make any sort of real money, he needed Gray off his back. After Gray declined an offer to work for Keating, in April 1987 the FHLBB chairman was summoned to Washington, D.C., to meet with Senators Dennis DeConcini (D) and John McCain (R) of Arizona, John Glenn (D) of Ohio, and Alan Cranston (D) of California. Flying 3,000 miles to meet with four senators was unusual for anyone, but then again so was Keating's far reaching influence. Unbeknownst to Gray, the senators owed Keating a favor and this meeting appeared to be a payback for the all-expenses-paid political junkets to the Bahamas and the collective $1.3 million Keating had donated to their campaign war chests.[8]

During the meeting, the senators tried to convince Gray that the FHLBB's 10 percent restriction was wrong — but the chairman didn't budge. In his opinion, if they had a problem with the equity rule they could talk to the regulators.[9]

The senators agreed.

A week later, regulator Michael Patriarca and litigation director William Black of the San Francisco office of the FHLBB arrived in Washington to meet with the four senators. Only this time they were joined by Senator Donald Riegle (D) of Michigan who, coincidentally, was the chairman of the Senate Banking Committee. Although most citizens would struggle to line up a single congressman, Keating had the luxury of five. He was dealing with a full house.

Powered by the prestige of their office, the senators pleaded on Keating's behalf: take it easy, stop the investigations, and ditch the equity rule. Patriarca and Black couldn't believe what they were hearing — the meeting was surreal. Five United States senators were arguing for them to ignore the trespasses of Lincoln Savings and Loan, an institution that was flagrantly breaking the law. Like Gray, Patriarca and Black didn't budge. Regardless of the muscle, they would not ignore the ruse that was going on at Lincoln. In fact, they would continue their review of Lincoln and would also refer the case to the Department of Justice for criminal investigation.[10]

In July 1987 Gray's term ended. He was replaced by M. Danny Wall who had formerly served as Senator Jake Garn's chief of staff. Garn, you'll recall, was the coauthor of the 1982 Garn-St. Germain Act which had thrown open the doors for S&Ls to enter into risky investments. In a not-so-surprising twist of fate, it was Wall who had written the draft of the bill. Now the S&Ls had a handpicked player on their team.

Although observers would have assumed that safeguarding the investments of depositors should be first on his agenda, Wall decided to look out for Keating's welfare. The new boss further defined his position by removing Patriarca and Black from the case. Then in September he brought in Darrel Dochow from Seattle to run the Office of Regulatory Affairs (ORA). One of Dochow's first assignments — per Wall — was to call San Francisco and have them delay a planned audit of Lincoln Savings and Loan.[11]

Three weeks later, Dochow met with Wall and Keating, who suggested the review be given to other investigators. Dochow took the hint, but his assistants reached a conclusion Keating didn't expect: the S&L was a "ticking time bomb" and the government should take control of the thrift.[12]

Wall and board member Roger Martin considered the recommendation, then dismissed it. Instead, they decided to conduct a year of private negotiations with Lincoln executives.[13] Wall defended his actions and later explained to *Time* magazine that San Francisco regulators had reputations for being "hysterical, over-zealous, and swept away by smoke where there is no gun."[14]

In the meantime, Dochow met with Keating's lawyer who requested the dispute be moved from San Francisco to Seattle, Dochow's former district. The change of venue, Keating assumed, would find the trespasses of his financial empire reviewed by friendlier forces.[15] Seattle objected to the unwarranted request. Not only would their caseloads be swamped if they had to review Lincoln's suspicious business dealings, it would also affect the independence of all regulators.

Dochow was undeterred. In an unprecedented move, he proposed that his own office, the Office of Regulatory Affairs in Washington, D.C., take over the investigation. In May 1988 the proposal was accepted by a 2-to-1 vote and Keating received a two-year reprieve.[16] Adding to Keating's victory was an agreement between Dochow's group and Lincoln Savings that the ORA could not review documents from prior investigations compiled by the San Francisco examiners.[17]

The extension was welcome news for the banker, who continued to spend his time spending other people's money. During the delay and confusion, he managed to mismanage the investments of clients by selling them $250 million worth of junk bonds in his own company. Keating's sales practices were unusual to say the least. In a 1987 memo to his American Continental Corporation bond sales staff, he wrote: "Remember, the weak, meek and ignorant are always good targets."

Despite a series of missteps and mistakes on the part of Dochow's Washington-based regulators, the investigation finally came to a head in April 1989. Regulators confirmed that Lincoln Savings and Loan was operating well outside established boundaries and, therefore, the government should take over the thrift. By the time the feds announced the takeover, two years of delays and Keating's unethical business practices had generated an unnecessary $1.3 billion in losses.

Now it was time for Keating to play his trump card. Although he controlled a $6.9 billion empire, he filed for Chapter 11 bankruptcy.[18] The move accomplished two things: it infuriated the feds who, at long last, seized the bank; and it gave Keating breathing room. He was now safeguarding assets which he claimed included land, securities, and other assets that were actually owned by Lincoln's various subsidiaries and not the bank itself.[19] Incidentally, the move also gave him rights to a $500,000 salary as the president of a corporation in Chapter 11.[20]

The government takeover also gave him an opportunity to draw upon his indignation, either real or imagined. Keating painted himself as a misunderstood patriot and declared it "an obscene thing to see a vigorous American enterprise destroyed and a caring family shattered."[21]

Back in Washington, Wall was finally ready to close the vault after the thieves had withdrawn the money. He was upset with Keating for placing subsidiary assets under bankruptcy protection, and was even more perturbed that Lincoln executives loaded boxes of documents into vans before the feds could seize the thrift.

Keating fought his way through a gauntlet of charges, perhaps the most notable being the $1.1 billion lawsuit filed by the Resolution Trust Corporation, the organization responsible for salvaging the remnants of the failed S&Ls. Meanwhile, the five senators who interceded on Keating's behalf had to undergo the public scrutiny created by their actions. Their embarrassment continued when Keating was asked if his contributions had influenced the five senators. The banker proudly replied, "I certainly hope so."[22]

The "Keating Five" were judged by peers who constituted the Senate Select Committee on Ethics. In March 1991 four of the five were absolved of any blame in extending Keating's run on the bank. Only Cranston was cited with "impermissible conduct." This may have been due to Cranston's bad timing. Unlike his colleagues, Cranston hadn't allowed enough time to lapse between receiving his cash prize and putting the pressure on regulators. Not surprisingly, the slap on the wrist the senators received convinced regulators that Keating's influence was still infiltrating congressional chambers.[23]

All this could have been avoided had S&L reforms been made earlier. But it was only after the 1988 elections that Congress gave any serious consideration to reforming the thrifts. Naturally, the change in policies and regulations were fought tooth and nail by the S&L lobbyists, who appeared on the verge of defeating any major changes until financier Warren Buffett protested by withdrawing his S&L from the U.S. League of Savings Institutions.[24] Eventually, the lobbyists caved and the way was cleared for reforms.

In the end, Keating (or "Mr. Cheating" as he was dubbed by his duped investors) had stolen the life savings of hundreds of investors and left taxpayers footing a $3.4 billion note. For this, he was convicted on 90 state and federal charges and sentenced to 12½ years in prison.

Despite the volume of lawsuits sparked by his financial atrocities, Keating's lawyers convinced the court that jurors at his 1993 federal trial had known too much of his past. Then they pointed out that the judge at his state trial (the infamous Lance Ito) had given improper instructions to the jury. Finally, his other criminal convictions were tossed out by the federal district court in Los Angeles. After serving roughly five years of his original sentence, Keating was released on bail in the fall of 1996. Unrepentant and unapologetic, the 73-year-old went to live with relatives and plan new business ventures.

Hmmm... would you buy a used anything from this man?

References

[1]Carlson, Margaret, "A Legal Bank Robbery," *Time*, Nov. 27, 1989, 29.

[2]Evans, Rowland, and Novak, Robert, "Who's To Blame For The Great S&L Scandal?," *Reader's Digest*, Apr. 1990, 66.

[3]Evans, Rowland, and Novak, Robert, op. cit., 67.

[4]Carlson, Margaret, op. cit., 29.

[5]Morganthau, Tom with Thomas, Rich, and Clift, Eleanor, 'The S&L Scandal's Biggest Blowout," *Newsweek*, Nov. 6, 1989, 35.

[6]Morganthau, Tom, et al., op. cit., 36.

[7]Ibid.

[8]Morganthau, Tom, et al., op. cit., 35.

[9]Morganthau, Tom, et al., op. cit., 36.

[10]Ibid.

[11]Adams, James Ring, "How To Win Friends And Influence Regulators," *National Review*, Mar. 19, 1990, 37.

[12]Evans, Rowland, and Novak, Robert, op. cit., 66.

[13]Adams, James Ring, op. cit., 37.

[14]Carlson, Margaret, op. cit., 29.

[15]Adams, James Ring, op. cit., 37.

[16]Ibid.

[17]Adams, James Ring, op. cit., 38.

[18]Kerwin, Kathleen, "For Charles Keating, The Best Defense Is A Lawsuit," *Business Week*, May 1, 1989, 32.

[19]Ibid.

[20]Morganthau, Tom, et al., op. cit., 35.

[21]Kerwin, Kathleen, op. cit., 32.

[22]Evans, Rowland, and Novak, Robert, op. cit., 69.

[23]Carlson, Margaret, "Then There Was One," *Time*, Mar 11, 1991, 69.

[24]Evans, Rowland, and Novak, Robert, op. cit., 70.

ALDRICH AMES
"The Traits of a Traitor"

This tale of intrigue and espionage may seem a bit out of place with our other stories of financial misadventure. But a closer look reveals startling similarities in the motivations (greed) and management reaction (denial) that plagued the subjects of our other stories. It would not be hard to imagine the scenario playing forth with a dishonest employee selling trade secrets to a corporate competitor rather than a rival Cold War superpower — but the lessons are the same.

In this case, Aldrich Ames proved you don't need much intelligence to be a mole within the Central Intelligence Agency (CIA). Despite the fact that he was sloppy, bitter, unorganized, and obvious, it took several years for his superiors to accept that there was a traitor in their midst. It took even longer to catch him.

● ●

Aldrich Ames may not have been the CIA's first choice as a spy. When he was hired in 1962, it may have been because better-qualified candidates were being sent to Vietnam. Possibly, it could have been nepotism: his father had performed minor covert operations for the CIA in Burma. Or was it the summer job he held as a teenager at the CIA's training facility?

Regardless of why he was hired, Ames had always envisioned himself as a man of international intrigue. Now, at only 21 years old, his job at the CIA was secured and he could see his dream becoming a reality.

By the time he completed training in 1968, he sought a position in Asia to procure secrets for the United States. But an earlier psychological assessment suggested he wasn't suited for spy work, and the rookie officer was instead sent to Turkey to recruit foreign spies to work for the United States.

Ames was desperate to make an impression on his boss, and he did. Sadly, it was the wrong impression. The station chief in Ankara said that Ames was so inept at recruiting agents that he should never be sent out in the field again.[1] Although his lack of interpersonal skills wasn't an asset, the CIA didn't think that should preclude him from working his way into more sensitive positions.

The CIA provided Ames with Russian language lessons and later assigned him to Directorate of Operations, the branch in charge of covert missions. He was successful at handling the affairs of Soviet spies who had agreed to pass along information to the United States. On the other hand, Ames never got the hang of actually recruiting them — a distinct disadvantage in his job. By the early 1980s he was being passed over for promotions so regularly that when a position opened in Mexico City in the fall of 1981, he grabbed it.

The move didn't improve his downhill record at recruiting foreign spies, but it did coincide with the earliest signs of his dissatisfaction with both the CIA and the Reagan administration.[2] In his opinion, the agency had lost its direction and become obsessed with their single-minded focus on Nicaragua. It was clear to colleagues that Ames was losing faith. Yet in 1983, despite his drinking binges and tepid Mexico City record, he was named the Soviet branch chief in the counterintelligence division.[3] From his new position in Langley, Virginia, Ames would now have access to Department of State and Department of Defense information.

As his career was improving, his personal life was also changing. Ames divorced his first wife in favor of Rosario Dupuy, whom he had met in Mexico. After relocating to a Washington suburb, they set up house, drove a secondhand car, and, within a year, had racked up $35,000 in credit card debt.[4]

Staggered by money problems and disgruntled over the CIA's actions, Ames found comfort in drinking. All this added up to his fateful decision to turn traitor. Ames thought that by selling American secrets to the Soviets, he could earn just enough money to pay off debts to his ex-wife and his creditors.

Since his job description included recruiting foreign operatives to sell secrets to the United States, neither the CIA nor the FBI gave a second thought to his April 1985 meeting with Soviet embassy diplomat Sergei Chuvakhin.[5] But when Chuvakhin didn't show, Ames slammed back a few vodkas, walked into the Soviet Embassy, and handed a guard the names of three double agents in the Soviet Union. He also provided a page torn from a CIA directory (in which Ames highlighted his name) and a typewritten note requesting $50,000.

To his surprise, a week later the KGB delivered the funds and Ames was ready to divulge more secrets. Months later, he strolled past CIA guards carrying a bag filled with secret documents and the names of 10 Soviet spies who worked for the United States.[6] By now, Chuvakhin could see that Ames — mediocre Ames — would make a superior KGB mole within the CIA. Chuvakhin also realized that with the information Ames had already provided, there were some people back home who needed to be eliminated.

At CIA headquarters in Langley, Virginia, a perplexing mystery was unfolding. In the year following Ames's initial meeting with Chuvakhin, about 20 Soviet spies working for the CIA suddenly stopped providing reports. There was no more contact, no more information, and no microfilm stashed in hollow trees. The law of averages suggested that these spies weren't taking early retirement, but that their covers had been blown.

But by whom?

The CIA hierarchy was rattled, but they refused to accept that anyone within their walls could possibly divulge such sensitive information. How could it happen? Employees were thoroughly screened, background checks were made, and controls were so foolproof that it was virtually impossible for a mole to infiltrate their ranks.

Virtually impossible, however, doesn't mean absolutely impossible.

In the fall of 1985 CIA officials tried to flush out the source by transmitting false documents designed to elicit a response by the KGB. When nothing happened, the obvious conclusion was that the source was inside Langley headquarters. To prevent further leaks, in January 1986 the chief of the Soviet division in the CIA's Directorate of Operations established a highly classified "back room" where sensitive cases could be handled.

The only problem? Ames was granted access.[7]

Over the following year, Ames met with Chuvakhin more than a dozen times but neglected to provide reports on the results of his meetings. Still, the CIA remained oblivious to the idea that Ames had become a traitor.

In July 1986 Ames was transferred to the American Embassy in Rome to begin a three-year assignment. While there, Rosario started sporting expensive Italian fashions and Ames began wearing $1,500 suits and keeping appointments with KGB contacts with his new Rolex watch.[8]

Back in Langley, the super secret backroom operation had offered only a band-aid effect. Since senior officials at the Directorate of Operations considered the possibility of a mole infiltrating the system to be near zero, support for an in-depth investigation was either delayed or severely limited. In fact, it took more than a year to form a four-person task force to begin a formal internal investigation. Even then the work of the team headed by CIA veteran Jeanne Vertefeuille was made more difficult by misinformation being leaked by the KGB.

But the dead-end streets didn't end there. In 1988 the CIA combined Vertefeuille's team with another group who was searching for other moles within the agency. Soon, the focus of the special task force was divided among other cases.[9]

Had the CIA scrutinized the actions of the alcoholic Ames, they would have seen he was flying more red flags than the Kremlin. It was said on one occasion that he forgot a briefcase filled with classified documents on a subway train. Then at a Christmas party in Rome, he got so drunk he passed out in the gutter and had to be carried home.[10]

But his boldest statement was made when the $70,000-per-year employee purchased a new Jaguar with funds he had received from his Soviet connections. Returning to the United States, he continued this lavish lifestyle by parking his Jag in the driveway of his new $540,000 house. The fact that there was no mortgage on the home made this an even more visible clue, but those on the trail of the mole assumed Rosario's wealthy family had bought it with cash.[11]

In September 1989, 29-year-old CIA investigator Dan Payne was working on ways to catch the traitor. Another CIA employee, Diana Worthen, noticed Ames's instant wealth and became suspicious — she knew that Rosario did not come from a wealthy family. Now all Payne had to do was follow the money and the trail would lead to the mole.

While Ames may not have had a conscience, he did have luck. Two months into Payne's investigation, the young agent was reassigned to a training course, followed by a temporary assignment overseas. With the investigation sidetracked, his unusual spending habits still didn't attract the suspicion of the CIA's upper echelon. Instead, the decision makers appointed him to the counterintelligence center — the division responsible for ferreting out moles.[12]

In his new position, Ames was supposed to analyze KGB operations. This was perfect for the KGB. Through him, they could now access the locations and identities of double agents working for the United States and edit reports the CIA relied on to conduct American operations.[13]

But the end was in sight. Payne returned from overseas and asked to continue his investigation on Ames. Fortunately his request caught the attention of the new deputy chief of the counterintelligence center, Paul Redmond.

Redmond and Ames had had prior conflicts. He also believed Ames to be a lush and a loser and immediately suspected he was the mole. Redmond and Vertefeuille approached the FBI to initiate a joint effort to expose the traitor.

In November 1991 Ames was finally interviewed regarding what he knew about the loss of agents in 1985. He admitted he had once left a safe open and, maybe, that's what happened. Someone got into the files and forwarded some sensitive information to the Soviets.[14]

Although the excuse sounded good to Ames, it sounded like a lie to Redmond. But Redmond's opinion didn't matter much to Ames.

The following month, bolder than ever, Ames traded his older Jaguar for a new XJ6, which he blatantly drove to work every day. Redmond and Vertefeuille saw that Ames was adding fuel to the fire.[15]

With a joint CIA/FBI effort underway, Payne was given access to Ames's financial records. He learned that Ames and his wife were racking up nearly $30,000 a month in credit card bills, but now they were paying them off on time.

Payne also found that over the last several years, Ames had received wire transfers of around $1 million and cash deposits of more than $500,000.[16] Then in October 1992, CIA employee Sandy Grimes compared Ames's deposits with his 1985 and 1986 meetings with Chuvakhin and found a match. They knew they had their man.[17]

Finally, in May 1993, the FBI placed Ames and his wife under surveillance, tapping their phones, sifting through their trash, bugging their cars, and downloading data from his computer. After acquiring enough information to prove Ames was the mole, in February 1994 they set up a roadblock and arrested him. It was just in time. Ames had been scheduled to fly to Russia the next day.[18]

Two months later Ames pleaded guilty and was sentenced to the maximum-security federal prison in Allenwood, Pennsylvania. Rosario was given five years.[19]

All told, at least 10 of the people Ames exposed were executed. He was paid or promised well over $4 million plus land in Russia in exchange for the delivery of thousands of documents and computer disks, the contents of which will forever remain a mystery to the American government.[20]

Back at the CIA, there was one thing missing in the flurry of finger pointing: accountability. No one was fired and only 11 reprimands were issued, which suggested that although the CIA needed a thorough housecleaning, the new director was content to dust floors.

Ames still wasn't satisfied. In a spectacular show of unmitigated gall, the traitor issued an international appeal to Russian journalists and others to join him in a lawsuit against United States' officials, claiming that the CIA reads and censors his mail.

But there's one sentence the CIA won' touch — his life sentence.

References

[1]Shannon, Elaine, "They Wouldn't Know A Mole If It Bit Them," *Time*, Oct. 24, 1994, 49.

[2]Corn, David, "A Talk With Aldrich Ames," *The Nation*, Sept. 11, 1995, 240.

[3]Earley, Pete, "The Price of Treason," excerpt from "Confessions Of A Spy, *U.S. News & World* Report, Feb. 17, 1997, 30.

[4]Ibid.

[5]Shannon, Elaine, op. cit., 49.

[6]Pound, Edward T., and Cohen, Gary, "The Spy Who Picked The CIA's Pockets," *U.S. News & World Report*, May 9, 1994, 49.

[7]Shannon, Elaine, op. cit., 49.

[8]Earley, Pete, op. cit., 34.

[9]Wise, David, "The Ames Spy Hunt," *Time*, May 22, 1995, 54.

[10]Shannon, Elaine, op. cit., 49.

[11]Wise, David, op. cit., 58.

[12]Ibid.

[13]Ibid.

[14]Ibid.

[15]Ibid.

[16]Ibid.

[17]Ibid.

[18]Ibid.

[19]Corn, David, op. cit., 238.

[20]Wise, David, op. cit., 55.

SUMITOMO
"Yasuo Hamanaka and the Copper Caper"

Some people have the good fortune to find the perfect job. For 48-year-old Yasuo Hamanaka, it was trading nonferrous metals — copper, to be specific — for Sumitomo, one of the largest trading companies in the world. For 10 years, he relied on his reputation as a tough trader to affect the cost of copper and bend prices at will. But there were two sides to Hamanaka's trading practices — one for each set of books he used to conceal the $2.6 billion he lost during a decade of deception.

• •

Depending on the personality Yasuo Hamanaka wanted you to see, he was either a quiet, unassuming man who lived in a modest home outside Tokyo, or an aggressive, influential trader who could buy a billion dollars worth of copper without batting an eye.

It had all been too easy for Hamanaka. Unlike Daiwa's Yoshihide Iguchi, the star trader who had risen through the company ranks despite an absence of promise, Hamanaka demonstrated skills that suggested rich rewards to the corporation fortunate enough to hire him. In 1970 he earned a law degree from Tokyo's respected Seikei University, but his legal career took a turn in 1972. He was hired by Sumitomo Corp., a blue-chip trading company and one of the largest players in the metals market, to work in their copper metals division.

Copper didn't offer the same sex appeal as gold or silver, but it didn't matter, really. Hamanaka had knowledge of the business and an unparalleled devotion to his company. For years he was content to be just a minor cog in a major machine. In 1985 his allegiance was rewarded: Hamanaka was promoted to trader and would now be responsible for trading copper futures and physical copper. He continued to rise through the ranks. In 1995 he was promoted again to general manager of the entire copper division.

After more than two decades, he was due. In the entire world, few shared Hamanaka's grasp of trading copper. From his simple metal desk in Tokyo, all it took was a nod of his head to sell a billion dollars worth of copper through the futures pits of New York and London — although Hamanaka rarely wanted to sell. Instead, the aggressive hustler had his eyes on a bigger prize. If he was smart (and he knew he was), he could corner the market and create a copper cartel. With time and Sumitomo's money on his side, all he had to do was stockpile his mountain of copper in exchange warehouses and bet it all when the odds were in his favor. Year after year, his mastery of manipulating the market helped him build up enough surpluses to prompt a supply squeeze and drive up the price of copper stock for other buyers. To the satisfaction of his employer, he was also driving up profits for Sumitomo.

It was this kind of fast-paced, profit-motivated thinking that was creating the legend of Yasuo Hamanaka. In his quest to corner the market, it was said that at one point he had acquired 16 percent of the world's share of copper, although modesty prevailed and he was given the nickname of "Mr. 5 Percent." Hamanaka's opinions were so revered, he could direct the vast $1.45 trillion market with just a rumor that he may be considering a purchase or a sale.[1]

By 1996 the 48-year-old was the undisputed king of the copper mountain. While Sumitomo's other traders had come and gone over the last two decades, Hamanaka's corporate piety and comprehension of copper had kept him in his bosses' favor. When he met with Sumitomo president Tomiichi Akiyama, Hamanaka spent 30 minutes discussing the intricacies of copper mining and how world events could affect the market. So while other executives were rotated to new positions, Hamanaka stayed put. His knowledge was one of Sumitomo's most valued assets.[2]

The salaried employee also shared the intangible benefit of the Japanese style of "trust-based" management. This honor system allowed Hamanaka the power to run his department on his terms — which Sumitomo assumed was honestly, efficiently, and effectively.

As far as his ultraconservative managers could tell, Hamanaka was on top of things. After 20 profitable and scandal-free years, they realized they could trust him implicitly. During the last 10 years, he had never taken a vacation; he stayed at work until 3 a.m. to monitor the New York commodity markets; and he was modest about his successes, yet aggressive when it came to making money for Sumitomo.[3] He wore inexpensive suits, owned a simple Mitsubishi, and rode a train home to his wife and two kids in a suburb outside Tokyo.

Yet this ordinary man was an extraordinary trader. Sumitomo bought and sold a half-million tons of copper each year, and Hamanaka's dealings regularly doubled or quadrupled the amount handled by other traders. He could locate and buy huge supplies of copper, leaving smaller companies scrambling to pick up the scraps he left behind.[4]

It seems Hamanaka's only weak points were conducting unauthorized trades, losing money in the process, and stealing funds to pay his tabs.

As head of the copper trading division, Hamanaka was granted unrivaled latitude in his authority. He had the power to sign his name to multimillion-dollar lines of credit on several bank accounts, authorize his own trades, and complete the paperwork when he was finished. Like Barings' Leeson and Daiwa's Iguchi, Hamanaka was omnipotent.

But not everyone trusted him. In 1991, as Hamanaka was building his copper empire, he was suspected of trying to fix the market. During an investigation into market manipulation at the London Metal Exchange (LME), his trading practices were closely scrutinized. As far as Hamanaka was concerned, "Coppergate" was probing a bit too close for his benefit. He wrote a letter on Sumitomo letterhead to New York-based copper broker David Threlkeld, asking him to provide backdated confirmations of a fictitious $425 million worth of trades.

In the letter, Hamanaka explained to his potential co-con-spirator that the forged documents "would not cause you any trouble/any damage/any loss at all." He also detailed ways Threlkeld could create a series of trades that were to have taken place in September 1990.[5]

Instead of helping Hamanaka, Threlkeld forwarded the letter and voiced his concerns to LME Chief Executive David King, who suggested that Threlkeld mind his own business and hope that Sumitomo didn't sue him. Sue him for what, Threlkeld wasn't certain.

Threlkeld kept his eyes on the red flag and asked his employees about suspicious trades conducted on Hamanaka's behalf. Two of them responded by leaving Threlkeld to open Winchester Metals, Ltd. Three years later, each was receiving $23 million annually, perhaps due to the large commissions being generated by their new client, Hamanaka. Threlkeld, meanwhile, found his fortunes waning as Sumitomo and others associated with Hamanaka refused to do business with him.[6]

The following year, Threlkeld himself raised the second red flag when he faxed the LME and Britain's Securities & Futures Authority (SFA) a series of letters advising them that huge amounts of business were taking place between a few brokers. This could hint at illegal prearranged sales, suggested Threlkeld. Again, the LME dismissed his warning. They advised Threlkeld that they had already looked into the matter and did not notice any suspicious activity.[7]

Sumitomo noticed the heavy trading as well, but took no immediate action. They did, however, make a halfhearted effort to strengthen controls by establishing a three-man team to look into their copper trading division. But the trio disbanded a year later, complaining of difficulties in obtaining account balances from Hamanaka's trading group.

Had they dug a little deeper, they would have known why Hamanaka was reluctant to part with any financial records. Apparently without Sumitomo's knowledge, he had borrowed $770 million from a subsidiary in Hong Kong and used the cash to buy nonexistent copper warehouse receipts to hide his losses from

Sumitomo. He repaid the loan with funds earned through derivatives that he had traded on a second set of books.[8]

But why were banks lending him money at all? In 1993 Hamanaka wrote to several brokers (again, on Sumitomo letterhead) and advised them Yasuo Hamanaka had the authority to move funds between Sumitomo accounts. But instead of signing his own name, he forged the names of two of his superiors.[9] To further cover his tracks, he also collected nearly $1 billion in loans in the form of derivative contracts from Chase Manhattan and J.P. Morgan Co.[10] And each month he falsified position statements from foreign brokers that he would provide to other back office officials.

Catching Hamanaka in the act of buying copper with money he didn't have should have been easy. In fact, he gave Sumitomo yet another chance to catch him in September 1993.

When copper prices began to rise inexplicably, outsiders suspected Hamanaka was controlling supplies. Hamanaka denied the allegations and explained that the huge purchases were ordered by Chinese buyers.[11] Sumitomo looked into the matter and realized Hamanaka's trades had exceeded his authorized ceiling, and the three investigative auditors were reinstated. Still, they could find nothing to confirm their suspicions. Once again, they disbanded.

If only they had examined the biggest clue in Hamanaka's caper and followed the metal.

The LME had already built storage warehouses in the Netherlands and Singapore, and in 1994 they built another mammoth facility in Long Beach, California. Within months, Sumitomo's copper holdings occupied almost 70 percent of the new warehouse space — a factor that was limiting supplies and artificially supporting prices.[12]

Red flag number six was showing its colors. Although the scam was escaping the notice of Sumitomo, it did attract the interest of Daniel Rappaport, chairman of the New York Mercantile Exchange (NYME).

Rappaport realized the LME warehouse was accepting huge shipments of copper, but little was being shipped out. Prompted by Rappaport's complaints, the U.S. Commodities Futures Trading Commission (CFTC) began an investigation to determine which traders housed enough copper in Long Beach to influence prices. They asked the LME. They quizzed British regulators. Neither responded.

Fortunately for the CFTC, Hamanaka's irregular trading practices were nothing if not consistent. In October 1995 he stopped trading through two metal trading groups and instead began operating primarily on the unregulated cash copper market. Allegations surfaced that he was once again fixing the market. This time the CFTC began examining Hamanaka's trading history and suspected he was involved in "backwardation," a practice whereby copper for immediate delivery costs more than copper for delivery two months out. Although backwardation is legal, it had regulators suspecting Hamanaka was controlling huge supplies of copper and artificially inflating its price.

For months, the CFTC prodded the LME and the British regulators to look into Hamanaka's practices. Although the LME kept silent, the stalemate with the British regulators began to thaw out during a snowstorm.

In January 1996 British regulators visiting Washington, D.C., were snowed in by a blizzard that closed the airports. With nothing else to do, CFTC officials killed time by emphasizing Hamanaka's suspicious activities. At long last, the British regulators agreed to investigate.[13]

By March, Britain's Securities and Investment Board had discovered numerous payments that even Sumitomo didn't recognize. They were hot on the trail, and the trail was leading to Hamanaka. The CFTC, meanwhile, joined in by notifying Sumitomo that two of their brokerage accounts were actually being operated by power of attorney through Global Minerals & Metals Corp. of New York. After considering the evidence, Sumitomo offered Hamanaka up to the CFTC for deposition.

After arriving at New York's Waldorf-Astoria in late April, Hamanaka was questioned and asked to appear at a second deposition in mid-June. On May 17, however, Sumitomo removed Hamanaka from his day-to-day copper trading activities — but not before praising his managerial abilities and suggesting he possessed the qualifications to become a company director.

That was one promotion Hamanaka would never see. His false accounts and attempts to corner the market were unraveling like a spool of thread. No longer head of the copper division, copper prices fell 6.4 percent. Add to that the resolution of a miners' strike in Chile, and the additional supply of copper drove prices down even further. And since he was no longer controlling the trading statements arriving from metal traders, "Mr. 5 Percent" could finally see light at the end of the tunnel.

Unfortunately, the light was out.

On June 5 a Sumitomo clerk noticed in a bank report that millions were being placed in a Sumitomo account known only to Hamanaka. So after 11 years of shuffling funds to finance his run on copper, there was no alternative but for Hamanaka to confess that the money was financing his purchases of copper and that he had been working with two sets of books for years.[14] It was probably no coincidence that the following day, copper prices fell an astounding 10 percent, which outsiders attribute to Sumitomo dumping tons of their copper holdings before announcing the scandal to the public a week later.[15] Although Sumitomo lost a few hundred million dollars on its copper stock, the financial beating only amounted to a bruised ego when compared to the company's $34.8 billion in assets.

Despite the earlier examples offered by Barings, Orange County, and Daiwa (a company Sumitomo had purchased after Toshihide Iguchi frittered away $1.3 billion), Sumitomo insisted it was caught completely off-guard by the actions of this solitary rogue trader. According to the company line, not a single person in this international conglomerate had a clue that Hamanaka was doing anything illegal. If that was the case, then Sumitomo's degree of naivete is unrivaled in modern history.

Unlike Leeson who could hide his losses on a computer, Hamanaka was dealing with a cache of copper that required an army of people to ship, transport, catalogue, and record. That small fact didn't seem to matter to Akiyama when he stepped before a bank of cameras and microphones and calmly explained to Tokyo reporters that "These transactions were made solely by Yasuo Hamanaka himself."

Akiyama also told a Japanese newspaper that over the past decade, Hamanaka had kept a secret set of books cataloguing $20 billion worth of unauthorized trades — roughly $12 billion more than Sumitomo had conducted legally in 1995.[16] So how did he do it? Simple. According to Akiyama, Hamanaka had all bank documents connected with the unauthorized dealings sent directly to him rather than to the company's financial department.

Management's excuse to hang it on Hamanaka may have sounded plausible at first, but he wasn't controlling all his trades. Other workers carried out his orders and almost certainly would have recognized unusual deals. Likewise, internal auditors had years to investigate and did not detect any deviations. In addition, the London Metal Exchange had been a lightning rod due to their lax regulations and unwillingness to enforce rules. In the 1980s tin and aluminum trading scandals nearly put LME out of business.[17] Sumitomo, some argued, should have recognized that LME's atmosphere was ripe for fostering and harboring rogue traders.

If those warnings weren't enough for Sumitomo, they only had to recall another copper scandal that had foreshadowed Hamanaka's ruse. A year earlier, a Chilean trader had lost roughly $200 million of the government's money while working with LME. Representing Chile's government-owned copper company, Codelco, the trader accepted payoffs from LME brokers to give a share of the company's business to selected firms.[18]

In October 1996 Hamanaka was arrested and pleaded guilty to all charges against him, including fraud and forgery. He also implicated a 1985 partner who he said helped him conduct his first unauthorized transaction.

The following spring, Yoshio Takeuchi, the head of Sumitomo's metals-trading internal controls division, explained that the company had known as early as 1992 that there were problems in the control system. He maintained that the scandal might have been avoided had Sumitomo shared responsibilities among copper traders and hired additional employees to verify trades.[19]

Takeuchi reasoned that Sumitomo's weak link was Hamanaka's reputation, experience, and knowledge of the market. Since he knew better than anyone how to navigate the market, Sumitomo executives had looked upon him with blind trust.

Things didn't work out so well for president Akiyama, either. After he resigned in February, shareholders filed a lawsuit against him and four other former Sumitomo officials for negligence in allowing Hamanaka to operate unchecked.

The damages?

$1.6 billion.

Just a billion shy of what Hamanaka lost.

References

[1]Shirouzi, Norihiko; Kanabayashi, Masayoshi; and McGee, Suzanne, "Market Struggles To Sort Out Sumitomo Mess," *Wall Street Journal*, Jun. 17, 1996, C3.

[2]Ibid.

[3]Yoder, Stephen Kreider; Sapsford, Jathon; Vogelstein, Fred; Frank, Stephen E.; and Behrmann, Neil, "Sumitomo Says Unauthorized Dealings In Copper Caused $1.8 Billion In Losses," *Wall Street Journal*, Jun. 14, 1996, A3.

[4]Shirouzi, Norihiko, et al., op. cit., C3.

[5]McGee, Suzanne, and Frank, Stephen E., "Sumitomo Debacle Is Tied To Lax Controls By Firm, Regulators," *Wall Street Journal*, Jun. 17, 1996, A5.

[6]Ibid.

[7]Ibid.

[8]Steiner, Robert, "Sumitomo Files New Complaint Against Hamanaka," *Wall Street Journal*, Nov. 12, 1996, A4.

[9]McGee, Suzanne; Frank, Stephen E.; and Shirouzu, Norihiko, "Japanese Authorities Arrest Key Figure In Sumitomo's Copper-Trading Debacle," *Wall Street Journal*, Oct. 23, 1996.

[10]McGee, Suzanne; Frank, Stephen E.; and Kahn, Joseph, "CFTC Probes Unusual Loans To Sumitomo," *Wall Street Journal*, July 23, 1996, A2.

[11]McGee, Suzanne; Frank, Stephen E.; and Kahn, Joseph, "Hamanaka May Have Inflated China Ties," *Wall Street Journal*, Jul. 1, 1996, A11.

[12]McGee, Suzanne, and Frank, Stephen E., op. cit., A5.

[13]Ibid.

[14]Ibid.

[15]McGee, Suzanne, and Frank, Stephen E., op. cit., A1.

[16]Ibid.

[17]lbid.

[18]Ibid.

[19]Staff Reporter, "Dow Jones Report," Mar. 19, 1997.

BANKERS TRUST
"Have We Got a Deal For You"

There are two ways to invest: you can either do it yourself or rely on the expertise of professionals. Although the do-it-yourself method may work for smaller investors, multimillion-dollar companies have to put their faith in financial institutions that specialize in finding safe havens for their fortunes. But faith wasn't enough to save the investments of two clients who lost millions through Bankers Trust-recommended derivatives.

• •

Bankers Trust was not your father's savings and loan.

Rather than accepting the domestic savings of the working class or retirement checks of senior citizens, the company focused on the highly profitable world of corporate and institutional finance, loan syndications, and international merchant banking. For nearly a century this approach had been a sound business policy.

Formed in 1903 to handle trust business for commercial banks, in just over a decade Bankers Trust had grown into an internationally recognized firm by buying out competing trusts. Eventually they expanded into securities and, after World War II, consumer banking. But Bankers Trust believed their real fortune lay elsewhere. In the late 1970s it was decided that Bankers would sell off their consumer banking business to focus on corporate services, primarily international commercial and merchant banking.

Things didn't work out as planned; there were a few false starts. By the late 1980s Bankers Trust needed to recoup profits so they turned to proprietary trading and risk management. The switch meant that clients willing to follow their advice would reap the rich rewards of... derivatives.

Unlike simple investments such as T-bills and stocks, derivatives allowed investors to hedge risks and bet on interest rates and currencies. Two major clients who agreed to the new direction were both Cincinnati-based businesses: Gibson Greetings, the card company who boasted $546 million in annual sales, and Procter & Gamble, the consumer-products legend.

Like Orange County Treasurer Robert Citron, Gibson and Procter & Gamble assumed derivatives would provide a safe and profitable haven for their investments. But the same torpedo that sank Citron's Orange County investments was now aimed at them.

In 1993, before the shot was fired, things were still calm. Bankers Trust was the seventh largest bank in America earning an annual net income of nearly $1 billion, a third of which was generated by derivatives. They were pleased to be twice as profitable as the average U.S. bank and many of their clients shared their success, notably, Gibson and Procter & Gamble.[1]

Earlier in the year, Procter & Gamble established an agreement with Bankers Trust to work with derivatives to lower their borrowing rate. By late November they had moved to a more complex product — a leveraged derivative that promised even lower interest rates.[2]

The investment worked as planned for the next few months, and on February 14, 1994, Procter & Gamble signed their third agreement. Neither Procter & Gamble nor Gibson Greetings uttered a discouraging word as long as they were receiving profits through this "miracle market."[3]

But things were about to change.

Two weeks earlier, on February 2, interest rates that had been descending for years got a boost from the Federal Reserve and, due to their interest-sensitive derivatives, the investments of several Bankers Trust clients went down.

Many investors accepted the loss, but vowed never to deal with complex derivatives again. Others mulled over the situation before taking action. Procter & Gamble and Gibson, on the other hand, had to face some hard facts.

Considering what had happened, could they believe what Bankers Trust was telling them... or selling them?

As far as Gibson was concerned, they were upset that when interest rates spiraled upward, Bankers Trust waited a few weeks before advising them that their prospective losses were unlimited. That left Gibson with two difficult choices. They could close out their account and wind up $17.5 million down or they could try to cap their losses by investing in another derivatives contract. Dazed by the potential liability, Gibson agreed to another contract to hold their losses at $27.5 million.[4]

In Procter & Gamble's case, the low interest rates they assumed they were receiving had now increased by 4.5 percent above commercial rates, which meant they now owed financing costs of more than $40 million.

If profits had clouded their vision, the eventual loss of $23 million (Gibson) and $157 million (Procter & Gamble) helped the blind to see.[5] Adding insult to injury, the matter became public knowledge because the derivatives hadn't been used as a hedge, but as speculation. The financial hit would have to be reported as a loss in quarterly statements.[6]

Suddenly, management was shouting for answers. Who authorized the purchases? Why was so much money shoveled into derivatives? Why didn't anyone create a contingency plan?

The questions may have come thick and fast, but the answers were few and far between. Now Procter & Gamble, Gibson, and several other Bankers Trust clients had to make a more sensible investment: attorneys.

In September 1994 Gibson filed a $73 million lawsuit against Bankers Trust, claiming they had provided false information and did not disclose the risk of derivatives.[7] Gibson argued that their initial derivatives deals had been simple, but Bankers Trust gradually led them to engage in riskier and more complex options.

Portraying the company and its financial staff as naive investors, Gibson claimed it had "little history or expertise in derivatives and no capacity independently to evaluate the benefits or risks involved."[8]

A month later Procter & Gamble followed their lead and filed its own lawsuit. This one, however, carried a $195.5 million price tag. Like Gibson, Procter & Gamble claimed that they were unsure what they were purchasing. From simple derivatives, they insisted Bankers Trust had talked them into buying more complex transactions intended to help them recoup their losses, but instead caused them to lose even more.[9]

In November 1994 Bankers Trust settled with Gibson by excusing all but $6.2 million of the fees it claimed it was owed.[10] The conciliatory gesture may not have been prompted solely by generosity, but by the discovery of a taped conversation between two Bankers Trust employees discussing ways to conceal the extent of Gibson's losses.

Procter & Gamble, however, continued to press the charge. They were given a boost in early December when the Securities and Exchange Commission, the Commodity Futures Trade Commission, and the Federal Reserve began preparing their own charges against Bankers Trust for securities, commodities, and banking violations tied into their derivatives activities. Without admitting or denying guilt, Bankers Trust agreed to pay a $10 million fine to settle charges that they had given Gibson inaccurate values for their derivatives.[11]

For Procter & Gamble, the real smoking gun was stashed within the walls of Bankers Trust. Like most organizations involved in capital markets, the corporation had installed a taping system that routinely recorded trading floor conversations to verify the accuracy of trades. Unfortunately, the practice proved to be as beneficial to them as the Watergate tapes were to the Nixon administration.

When Procter & Gamble got its hands on more than 6,000 taped conversations and over 300,000 pages of documents that painted an unflattering portrait of the business practices behind Bankers Trust, the tables began to turn.[12]

In a videotaped training session obtained by Procter & Gamble, a Bankers Trust employee explains, "What Bankers Trust can do for Sony and IBM is get in the middle and rip them off — take a little money." The employee pauses, then adds — perhaps as an attempt at humor — "Let me take that back. I just realized I'm being filmed."[13]

Other incidents captured for posterity, however, were definitely lacking any trace of humor. Procter & Gamble cited an employee musing aloud, "Funny business, you know? Lure people into that calm and then just totally f_ _ _ 'em."[14]

Procter & Gamble had more ammo in reserves. They claimed the criminal culture ran so deep at Bankers Trust, the acronym R.O.F. (for "rip-off factor") showed up in corporate conversations and documents, such as one allegedly showing a "7 (basis point) rip-off factor" on a deal that would net Bankers Trust $1.6 million.

Bankers Trust, logically, took the opposite tack. They pointed out that Procter & Gamble was a sophisticated investor and they knew what they were getting into when they entered the derivatives market. They released their own transcripts that revealed a conversation with a Bankers Trust representative explaining derivatives to a Procter & Gamble treasury employee.

Procter & Gamble countered by disclosing more transcripts in which Bankers Trust employees remark that the new contract "could be a massive, huge, future gravy train."[15] The comment wasn't far from the truth, considering the derivatives contract Procter & Gamble signed on November 2, 1993, carried with it an exit penalty clause — a penalty that increased in costs even as interest rates dropped. By the time Procter & Gamble locked in interest rates in April 1994, their financing costs had risen to $195.5 million.[16]

Procter & Gamble continued to insist this was standard operating procedure for Bankers Trust. Taking note of the treatment other Bankers Trust clients received, Procter & Gamble concluded that the defendant would coax clients into purchasing complex derivatives for additional gains (or to protect themselves against further losses). The practice was all but confirmed by a trader musing over a client's haphazard portfolio.

"If this ever comes out in the press, it is the most insane mess of trading I've ever, ever seen... they just keep trying to trade them out of losses."[17]

Again, Bankers Trust retaliated by reversing the blame. They insisted that instead of Procter & Gamble correcting their internal investing problems, they were more anxious to enter a legal battle. While former Bankers Trust employees agreed to provide full disclosure on transaction terms, they were purposely coy about the risks involved.

With each party trying to out-pity one another, Richard Breeden, the former head of the Securities and Exchange Commission, observed that the "starting obligation is with management to take prudent steps to manage controls, to prevent financial risks beyond its ability to absorb."

Unfortunately, Breeden's words of wisdom came too late for Procter & Gamble whose investments were lost in the black hole of complex derivatives — a product that could even baffle the traders selling them.

The suit took an even nastier turn when Procter & Gamble tacked on RICO (racketeer-influenced and corrupt organization) charges, claiming the tapes proved Bankers Trust was involved in a "pattern of mail, wire, and securities fraud..." Bankers Trust saw the move as a thinly veiled attempt at blackmail.[18]

Although the matter was eventually settled out of court, Procter & Gamble felt they had won their battle, but in doing so they had to publicly admit they were ignorant of derivatives and the risks involved — a tactic usually reserved for small investors. In 1996 Bankers Trust agreed to absorb up to $150 million of Procter & Gamble's derivative losses.

The fiasco also initiated safety features for investors. Rather than baffle investors with complex, weird formulas that make up derivatives, Bankers Trust was ordered to provide clients with daily prices on their derivatives.

Considering the potential dangers involved in derivatives, who can tell if even full disclosure can protect an investor from the risks?

Or the half-truths of traders?

References

[1]Levinson, Marc, "Exiled On Wall Street," *Newsweek*, Nov. 14, 1994, 49.

[2]Holland, Kelley; Himelstein, Linda; and Schiller, Zachary, "The Bankers Trust Tapes," *Business Week*, Oct. 16, 1995, 110.

[3]Holland, Kelley, et al., op. cit, 108.

[4]Lipin, Steven, "Bankers Trust Sued On Derivatives," *Wall Street Journal*, Sep. 11, 1994, C1.

[5]Ibid.

[6]Levinson, Marc, op. cit., 50.

[7]Lipin, Steven, op. cit., C1.

[8]Levinson, Marc, op. cit., 49.

[9]Lipin, Steven, op. cit., C1.

[10]Lipin, Steven, "Gibson Greetings Reaches Accord In Suit Against Bankers Trust Over Derivatives," *Wall Street Journal*, Nov. 25, 1994, A2.

[11]Lipin, Steven and Taylor, Jeffrey, "Bankers Trust Settles Charges On Derivatives," *Wall Street Journal*, Dec. 23, 1994, C1.

[12]Holland, Kelley; Mmelstein, Linda; and Schiller, Zachary, "The Bankers Trust Tapes," *Business Week*, Oct. 16, 1995, 106.

[13]Holland, Kelley, et al., op. cit., 1O8.

[14]Ibid.

[15]Ibid.

[16]Ibid.

[17]Ibid.

[18]Holland, Kelley, et al., op. cit., 107.

CITIBANK
"From Russia,
With Looting"

The automation of banking has provided an unparalleled level of convenience to everyone who uses it. Computerized automatic withdrawals enable customers to pay their utility, telephone, insurance, and mortgage payments without ever setting foot in a bank lobby. But the reliance on computers has proven to be a double-edged sword. Citibank found this out when Russian computer hacker Vladimir Levin infiltrated their once-secure system to arrange millions of dollars in unauthorized withdrawals — without ever setting foot in the United States.

• •

Most corporations have accepted the unpleasant fact that some employees will steal. Whether it's on the multimillion-dollar scale of Joseph Jett or merely the nickel and dime pilfering of hourly employees, internal theft has prompted corporations to build what they hope will be foolproof security systems.

With luck, the protective measures will catch dishonest employees, but what happens when the criminals work outside the company? Or even worse — outside the country? It's a nightmare for any corporation. And Citicorp lived it.

It was the summer of 1995 when a South American investment banker looked at his computer and noticed something was awry. Argentinean funds were being diverted to New York and then on to San Francisco via Citicorp computers.[1] Normally this wouldn't have been a problem, but none of the transfers were authorized. That meant that someone, somewhere in the world, had cracked Citicorp computer codes and was busy building a complimentary nest egg.

The accounts of corporate customers — one of the most fiercely protected domains in banking — were under attack by a hacker. With more than half a trillion dollars a day being transferred electronically, the potential loss would dwarf that of Daiwa, Barings, Sumitomo, and Orange County combined.[2]

Had it been a matter of a rogue employee, internal auditors would only have to peel back layer after layer of lies, deception, and cover-ups to expose the thief. But a 1994 internal investigation had already determined that hackers were finding it easier to break into Citicorp's system. That meant Citicorp would have to launch a painstaking global search to find an anonymous thief hidden within a worldwide electronic network. This prompted Citicorp to call the FBI.

Citicorp was determined to catch the hackers — wherever they were. Like a hunter lying in wait for his prey, by July Citicorp had created a New York headquarters from which they could watch any suspicious transfers. At first, the waiting game was monotonous. But a month later, the hacker appeared online.

From an Invest Capital account in Buenos Aires, $200,000 was being moved through a Citicorp computer to five recently opened accounts in San Francisco. As a bank official in Buenos Aires watched the funds evaporate, he realized there was absolutely nothing he could do to stop the illegal transaction. His bank was being robbed in cyberspace.

Helpless, the banker called the authorities and alerted Citicorp. The corporation traced the withdrawals and subsequent deposits to San Francisco and notified the bank to freeze the accounts. Citicorp then placed a second call — to the San Francisco headquarters of the FBI.

When Katerina Korlokov arrived at Sumitomo Bank the next day, she informed the teller she wished to withdraw funds from an account she had opened only weeks earlier. Korlokov didn't know the teller had been tipped off. When he explained the $31,000 she requested had been transferred into her account fraudulently, Korlokov left. A day later, FBI agents armed with a warrant for her arrest found Korlokov with a one-way ticket to Russia.[3]

Despite her arrest, the criminals maintained a synchronized schedule. While FBI agents were reading Korlokov her rights, halfway around the world another partner in crime was busy opening five new accounts in Israel. A short time later, the hacker once again broke into Citicorp computers and shuffled nearly $1 million from the Bahamas to the Israeli banks.[4]

By now, Citicorp had time and the FBI on their side. The following day when Palmidis Alexios arrived in Tel Aviv to withdraw $188,000, Israeli police were waiting to arrest him.

At this point the hacker had two strikes against him, but he wasn't out yet. In Rotterdam, Holland, Frans Bul called his bank to advise them a large deposit would soon be transferred to his account electronically. And, he added, he would need to withdraw that same amount in cash.

Seems the hacker had paid an electronic call on a Citicorp-affiliated Uruguayan bank and withdrawn $717,000 for deposit into Bul's account. Not content to stop there, the hacker added an additional $900,000 stolen from another Citicorp affiliate in Argentina.

Although the electronic transfers were no longer unusual to Citicorp, Bul received a big surprise when he was arrested while trying to make his multimillion-dollar withdrawal.

The police now had three accomplices, but no mastermind. Had the arrests scared the hacker? Would he simply drop out of sight? Hardly. Even masterminds have the fatal attraction of returning to the scene of the crime.

A month later, the hacker tried to move funds to Switzerland. His attempts were foiled when Citicorp froze the accounts. By now, more than 40 break-ins in five months made tracing the source of the transfers as easy as tracing a telephone call. Citicorp discovered the hacker was working out of St. Petersburg, Russia.[5]

Russian police agreed to check phone records and quickly tracked the transfers to the trading company AO Saturn.[6] Although the authorities knew where the transfers were coming from, they still had to find out who was making them. Their break came in December when Katerina Korlokov finally decided to cooperate with the FBI. She blew the whistle on a 28-year-old software developer named Vladimir (or Volodya) Levin, who was attempting to get rich quick at the expense of Citicorp.

Although they now knew the identity of the computer criminal, the FBI didn't stand a chance of taking Levin into custody. There was no extradition treaty between the United States and Russia, nor did Russian law specifically state that wire fraud in this case was illegal.

In February there was a glimmer of hope when the FBI learned that Levin and Korlokov's husband, Eugene, would be traveling outside Russia.

When Levin arrived in England on March 2, 1995, he was greeted by Scotland Yard. Since Korlokov had previously withdrawn funds from a Levin-manipulated account, he also received a similar reception from the FBI when he arrived in New York on March 10.[7]

Now there were bigger questions to answer. How had Levin accessed highly secured corporate accounts using nothing but a simple PC and the Sprint telephone network? How did he obtain passwords and user IDs?

His ability to achieve that and circumvent other electronic safeguards suggested to the FBI that he was working with someone inside Citicorp. Others argued that Russian hackers who can master their clunky secondhand computers can usually figure out clever shortcuts to break into more sophisticated, streamlined systems.[8] For instance, thousands of Russians were unable to afford Internet access through American Online, so hackers did it the easy way: they stole it.

In the end, over an 18-month period, Levin had juggled approximately $12 million in Citicorp customer accounts and walked away with a little more than $400,000.[9] Detained in England, Levin fought extradition. However, in August 1995 a British court ruled that there were sufficient grounds to send him to the United States.

As far as Citicorp was concerned, that was the first legal transfer Levin had ever made. By placing him before an American court, they would hopefully learn how he broke into their system. Whether Levin would level with them or not wasn't as important as what Citicorp learned: new ways to protect themselves from hackers who think they can bypass walls of electronic security to siphon off millions of dollars.

Following the Levin case, internal security measures were upgraded and passwords that hackers thought they could crack were programmed to change after each use.

But as Levin proved and Citicorp learned, electronic fraud continues to pose a threat to any organization. And as long as there are computers and hackers, you can bet they'll continue to baffle banks.

References

[1]Carley, William M., and O'Brien, Timothy L., "Cyber Caper How Citicorp System Was Raided and Funds Moved Around World," *Wall Street Journal*, Sept. 12, 1995, A1

[2]Ibid.

[3]Carley, William M., and O'Brien, Timothy L., op. cit., A18.

[4]Ibid.

[5]Ibid.

[6]Carley, William M., and O'Brien, Timothy L., op. cit., A1.

[7]Carley, William M., and O'Brien, Timothy L, op. cit., A18.

[8]Caryl, Christian, "Russia's Hackers: Reach Out And Rob Someone," *U.S. News & World* Report, Apr. 21, 1997, 58.

[9]Holland, Kelley, "Bank Fraud, The Old-Fashioned Way," *Business Week*, Sept. 4, 1995, 96.

THE GREAT PYRAMIDS OF EASTERN EUROPE "The Return of Charles Ponzi"

When 70 years of Communist rule ended in the late 1980s, millions of Eastern Europeans were eager to taste the fruits of capitalism. Looking to America for direction, some entrepreneurs opened small businesses, while others had bigger ideas. They opted to import an American concept known as the Ponzi scheme, a volatile get-rich-quick pyramid scam that claimed to turn small investments into huge profits. When Romanian investors lost their life savings, they took it in stride. When Albanian investors realized they had been fleeced, they took their country to the brink of civil war.

● ●

Until the late 1980s, life went on without too many surprises in Eastern European countries such as Albania and Romania. Although Communism had crushed independent thought, at least it provided some degree of consistency. The party dictated where you worked, the hours you worked, and how much you would be paid.

But then communism began to fall apart. Suddenly, millions found themselves in an unusual position. With capitalism, they were given unlimited opportunities to make money. Some chose to do it the easy way by investing in organizations that promised returns as high as 1,000 percent. What they didn't realize was that these organizations were updated versions of a scheme named in honor of America's most notable con man, Charles (Carlos) Ponzi.

Turn back the clock to Boston in 1920. The small-time crook noticed American and Italian postage stamps were of different values, yet both provided sufficient postage to send mail between the countries. And since World War I had devastated the economies of several smaller European countries, the difference in values was even greater. Ponzi had an idea.

He would purchase thousands — no, *millions* — of postal reply coupons from poor nations, bring them to America, sell them, and earn a yield as high as 400 percent per coupon. With this pretzel logic, Ponzi suggested that savvy investors could join him and earn a fortune by purchasing his 'Postal Union Coupons.' In just 45 days they would receive a 50 percent return, doubling their money in only three months.[1]

Within months, Ponzi's official-sounding Securities Exchange Company had reaped nearly $10 million from 10,000 investors who purchased the promissory notes. Ponzi and a select few investors made a killing during the first few weeks. But soon it was harder to find ground-floor investors to generate the profits already promised to those approaching the top of the financial "pyramid."

With less than a penny profit on each coupon, Ponzi would have to ship millions of postal reply coupons to the United States to make the sort of money he had promised investors. Even then, postal officials had limited the number of coupons that could be exchanged to a maximum of 10.[2]

Six months after the first 'Postal Union Coupon' was sold, there were no more investors to keep the scam alive. Ponzi's pyramid crumbled. Sentenced to federal prison, he was released long enough for his lawyers to work on an appeal. That gave Ponzi just enough time to flee to Florida, where he switched gears and started a real estate scam.[3]

Eventually Ponzi was caught, served a prison term, and ended up in Brazil, where he died a pauper. He may be gone, but the "Ponzi Scheme" continues through pyramid plans where investors are fooled by a switch in accounting semantics. Since thousands of people invest, ground-floor investors receive money which is not income but redistributed capital — money that the scam's organizers steal from Peter to pay Paul.

It's safe to assume, however, that few Albanians or Romanians had ever heard of Ponzi or any other pyramid scam artists. Noticing their fellow citizens were ripe for a rip-off, con men (and, in some cases, con corporations) moved in to lure naive capitalists into get-rich-quick schemes.

In Romania, investors who hoped to supplement their average $60 monthly income were seduced by promises of some 500 pyramid schemes that sprang up in their country after communism collapsed. In particular, they were attracted to the city of Cluj, home of the investment known as Caritas, or 'Charity.'[4]

Started in 1992 by accountant Ion Stoica, Caritas promised investors a chance to earn a 1,000 percent return within three months. In a country where hope is as scarce as cash, Stoica's "financial mutual assistance circuit" (a title worthy of Ponzi himself) gave four million depositors their chance at the brass ring.

For more than a year, Caritas was flying high on money collected from nearly 20 percent of the country's population. Its organizers claimed to have created 80,000 millionaires, a statistic that is less impressive when you consider one million Romanian leu is equivalent to only about $1,000.

As in any pyramid scheme, investors who got in when Caritas began in April 1992 had a chance to recoup their capital and earn a tidy profit. But within 18 months, friends, relatives, and acquaintances who were lured into the scam were unknowingly supporting the nouveau riche sitting atop the pyramid. They didn't realize it, but their chance to strike it rich had already struck out.

In the meantime, other low-rung investors who didn't grasp the instability of the scam ignored work while awaiting their cash cow. With millions of hopeful people idled and instant millionaires living it up, the city of Cluj experienced the highest inflation in Romania.

Regardless, the city's fragile economy didn't seem to affect the local government. The mayor received campaign contributions from Caritas and the community accepted donations for public statues and improvements. City officials also received another Caritas perk: their share of the take before other investors.

But even that didn't stop people from traveling to Cluj to get a piece of the action. Nor did it stop disgruntled investors from making the trip to recover their initial investment. But by the fall of 1993, the demise of Caritas was in sight. Company officials began downplaying promises of rewards and told investors the smaller dividends would be distributed once a month — if at all.

Eventually Caritas followed the destiny of other pyramid scams and faded away, taking with it $1 billion collected from four million investors. Surprisingly, Stoica won again. He spent less than two years in prison for the misuse of city funds.[5]

Like a phoenix, Ponzi schemes have a tendency to rise from the ashes as they have done in Russia, Bulgaria, Serbia, and the Czech Republic. Unfortunately, the schemes flourished in the neighboring country of Albania.

In 1992 Democratic Party candidate Sali Berisha ran for president, promising to introduce democracy and improve market economics. With me, Berisha pledged, everyone will win. To get his point across, Democratic Party campaign posters showed people driving luxury cars, enjoying beach vacations, and living in new homes. Fellow candidates took his lead and added not-so-subtle pyramid logos to their campaign literature.[6]

To his supporters, Berisha was an Albanian Moses who would lead them to the promised land of the West. He preached the gospel of free-market capitalism and European values. He also jockeyed for a spot in NATO and the European Union. Berisha won.

Years later, communism was a distant memory and Albanians were enjoying the curious offerings of capitalism. They were now investing in "foundations" which promised huge returns in just a few short months. Although they lived in the poorest nation in Europe, between 50 percent and 90 percent of the population invested a portion of their $100 average monthly salaries into a dozen pyramid schemes.[7] And why not? Wasn't this what capitalism was all about? Isn't this how people made money in the West? After all, they couldn't lose. These foundations were licensed by the government and, ergo, were backed by the government.

If investing money in these scams was the Albanians' first mistake, believing the government would cover their inevitable losses was their second.

The International Monetary Fund warned the Albanian government that the inevitable collapse of the pyramids would lead to chaos, but the warning was ignored and the pyramid investments continued. Naive Albanians withdrew money from their savings and accepted donations from relatives living abroad. Their average investments in the schemes totaled about $2,000 each. Overall, the foundation took in between $1 billion and $3 billion — a figure representing a huge portion of the country's personal savings.[8]

By January 1997 the Ponzi schemes were disintegrating and the organizers took off with the remaining funds. Slowly, word began to spread among millions of investors that the government didn't control or regulate the schemes. Realizing they had been cheated out of their money, investors organized peaceful protests throughout the country.

By February the government froze the assets of several foundations and returned a token sum to placate investors. Berisha considered printing more money to pay the bills but the treasury was too broke to cover the tab. As far as Berisha was concerned, there was only one other solution.

He tightened his grip on the country, dismissed the government, and had the parliament reelect him for another five-year term.[9] Suddenly, Albanians knew that losing their life savings was trivial compared to returning to a communist lifestyle. Southern Albanians who had previously made an illegal living smuggling merchandise to and from Italy noticed that they too had been scammed. Now everyone's fury was redirected at Berisha, who they suspected was the mastermind behind the pyramids.

Angry mobs attacked government officials and vandalized government buildings, to which Berisha responded by sending out troops to arrest the protesters. But the protesters were determined. They began blowing up bridges, taking over police stations, and looting military arsenals for antitank and antiaircraft missiles. Some disgruntled investors opened the doors of the jails and recruited prisoners into their makeshift army.[10] Killing was indiscriminate: citizens, secret police, and soldiers were wiped out.

By March the army and government collapsed and countries such as Italy and Germany began evacuating its citizens. Choppers from the U.S. Sixth Fleet dropped in to rescue Americans stranded in the capital city of Tirana. Anarchy quickly replaced order.[11]

It may have come too late, but in a final effort to restore peace, Berisha formed a commission to find the missing billions. But having maintained a hands-off attitude on the pyramid organizations, the government was out of luck.

Bowing to international pressure, Berisha called for special elections. Ironically, he lost to the leader of the Socialist Party.

In retrospect, it was inevitable. Like the financial schemes that took the life savings of his countrymen, Berisha's personal pyramid had also collapsed. He resigned on July 23, some six months after the protests began.

In the end, the scams had a dire effect on an unaware society and caused upheaval in both countries. Chances are good that the pyramids will again rise and crumble. Yet one fact remains the same: Ponzi's legacy will never die.

References

[1]Knutson, Mark C., 'The Remarkable Criminal Financial Career of Charles K. Ponzi," Charles K. Ponzi Website.

[2]Ibid.

[3]Ibid.

[4]Demick, Barbara, "Millions Of Romanians Swept Up In Get-Rich Scheme," *Knight-Ridder/Tribune News Service*, Dec. 1, 1993.

[5]Ibid.

[6]Nelan, Bruce W., "The Ponzi Revolution," *Time*, Mar. 17, 1997, 32.

[7]Staff Reporter, "Albania's House Of Cards," *The Economist*, Oct. 12, 1996, 81.

[8]Walsh, James, "Balkan War, Again: Albania's South Rises In Rebellion Against A State On The Brink Of Chaos," *Time*, Mar. 17, 1997, 32.

[9]Nelan, Bruce W., op. cit., 32.

[10]Walsh, James, op. cit., 32.

[11]Walsh, James, "No Law Or Order In The Land: Foreigners Flee As Tiny Albania Dissolves Into Mad Max-Style Chaos," *Time*, Mar. 24, 1997, 60.

Epilogue

The old saying "Fool me once, shame on you — fool me twice, shame on me" invites us to learn from our mistakes. When dealing with fraud, it is much less painful to learn from the mistakes of others. So what can we learn from the cases presented? Are there some common pearls of wisdom that will keep us from being "fooled again"?

Conventional wisdom concerning fraud suggests that two ingredients are necessary — need and opportunity.   The motivating factors underlying the need are greatly varied and open to debate, but with the exception of Robert Citron's Orange County fiasco (a case of executive hubris), the need appeared to be satisfied by money and/or the power associated with it.

This is perhaps not so surprising. What may be a bit more surprising is that direct theft only played a role in less than half the cases (Keating, Ames, Citibank, and the Romanian Ponzi scheme). The fraud in the remaining cases was much subtler. The traders at Bankers Trust and Prudential engaged in questionable sales practices; Joseph Jett falsified Kidder Peabody's trading records; Daiwa's Iguchi & Barings' Leeson hid extensive trading losses. What was the motivation? While it may never be possible to say for certain, all signs seem to point toward increasing or protecting compensation.

The implications of this approach are somewhat disturbing. Basic fraud prevention and detection is often directed toward securing assets and looking for red flags such as living beyond one's apparent means. However, since these cases involved authorized payments (salary & bonus) from legitimate sources (payroll) and were usually generous enough to support relatively lavish lifestyles, these two techniques are rendered decidedly less effective. For example, Joseph Jett's $9 million bonus was awarded by management, paid through conventional corporate systems, and could obviously support a highly extravagant lifestyle.   The fact was, however, that it was based on distorted records and fraudulent trades.

Moreover, highly paid employees sometimes fall prey to the star syndrome, where both themselves and, sadly, their management, believe their actions are above reproach.

Some needs may be fairly apparent (credit problems, substance abuse, gambling debts). Others may be more rooted in an individual's psyche (power, competition, status). While ideally we should be aware of people's needs and thereby intervene to prevent fraud, it is not practical to assume that we will have foreknowledge of the psychological state of all employees. We are left, therefore, to turn to a more practical element — reducing the opportunity.

Like the underlying need, the opportunities to commit fraud are highly varied. Nevertheless, from these seemingly dissimilar cases, there are some common elements. Most apparent was management failure. In the case of Daiwa and Charles Keating, management was an actual participant in the fraud. While management's contribution is not usually so blatant, in many of the other cases their actions or inaction had an equally devastating effect.

The most recurring theme seemed to be management's failure to supervise. A short time before the Orange County pension fund went bankrupt, one of Robert Citron's supervisors gave the following remark to a local newspaper concerning Citron's ability to produce unusually high investment results, " . . . I don't know how in the hell (Citron) does it, but it makes us all look good." Sky-high profits well beyond historical trends were never questioned at Barings or Paine Webber. In fact both Leeson and Jett were highly rewarded by a seemingly unwitting management and urged to continue.

Then there are the sins of omission. Whether management actually encouraged the questionable sales practices adopted by the traders of Bankers Trust and Prudential is unclear. What is apparent, however, is the absence of management's communication of their expectations for ethical behavior. Absent any other apparent motivation, it would not be unrealistic to assume that the reward structure adopted by management at least indirectly inspired such conduct. Managerial inertia was also evident by ignoring employee complaints of inappropriate behavior (Kidder

Peabody) and the failure to address identified control weaknesses (Barings, Daiwa).

Since management is ultimately responsible for the assignment of authority and responsibilities, we can also hold them accountable for the poor segregation of duties which played a key role in allowing Nick Leeson and Daiwa's Iguchi to cover their fraudulent trading activity.

But management is not to blame for everything. They did not force the ill-fated investments in the Romanian Ponzi schemes or coerce Procter & Gamble to undertake ridiculous deal structures with Bankers Trust. Here another powerful force seemed to be at work — greed. The law of risk and return suggests that greater reward can only be achieved by accepting greater risk. This is a fundamental tenet in business which can be more simply expressed by two well-worn clichés: "There is no such thing as a free lunch," and "If it looks too good to be true, it probably is." Unfortunately the most basic rule of caveat emptor[1] was forgotten in these two cases.

There are of course more specific fraud opportunities within each individual case. Iguchi did not take a vacation in his 11 years with Daiwa; Ames's lifestyle was clearly beyond his means; and Citron made a conscious decision to engage in risky investment strategies, inconsistent with the objectives of a pension fund.

Valuable lessons may be gained from these and all such misfortunes, but we must keep in mind that in these instances we have the gift of 20/20 hindsight. The true challenge is not understanding the circumstances surrounding past frauds, but in effectively using this information to prevent a similar occurrence. These situations provide an object lesson of what not to do, which in turn helps us in identifying potential fraud scenarios and supporting arguments for improvements. But if we fail to meet this challenge, if we are fooled again, then the shame would appropriately rest with us.

_____

[1] Let the buyer beware.